Aren't You Going To Taste It, Honey?

Mary Alice Powell's
Favorite Recipes From Over
40 Years As The Blade's Food Editor

With Introductions And Comments On Each Recipe
By Mary Alice Powell

Published By
THE BLADE
541 N. Superior Street
Toledo, Ohio 43660

Dedicated to the readers of The Blade food pages with appreciation for their steadfast loyalty.

Photography by Herral Long
Design by Bill Happel
Edited by Carol Block
Food styled by Mary Alice Powell

Library of Congress Catalogue Card Number 95-60024
ISBN 0-9614554-2-X

Foods pictured on the front cover: Strawberry Cheesecake Triffle, Fruit-Stuffed Crown Roast of Pork, Marinated Vegetables, Sour Cream Apple Pie, Marcy Kaptur's Polish Coffee Cake, Betty's Salad, and Belly Stickers.

Foreword

This book is a unique collection of 250 recipes selected by Miss Mary Alice Powell from the thousands she has tasted, perfected, and passed on to her readers for over 41 years as The Blade's food editor.

Many of the recipes reflect her pride in the native heartland cuisine of northwest Ohio. During several interviews and visits with Miss Powell, as well as working with her in the kitchen on special projects like the Disney World Chefs Team's visit to The Toledo Blade's Food Fair, I have found her to be a true food lover and passionate about investigative food journalism.

Therefore, this collection is representative of the home-grown recipes of the region, and her comments on each recipe is an historical review of America's eating habits and appliances over the past four decades. This work is sure to bring back memories to her longtime readers and become a valuable resource to budding cooks and chefs.

Its history truly reflects what makes American cuisine the most universally accepted and admired cuisine in the world today.

Keith Keogh, CEC, AAC
President, World Association of Cooks Societies
Manager, 1992-1996, Culinary Team USA

Preface

I am not sure if the world needs another cookbook. I only know that I desperately needed to write this one, for the readers of The Blade and for myself. It's a culmination of more than 41 years of writing recipes for The Toledo Blade, one of America's great newspapers.

Being a food editor is far more than writing a recipe. The title, "Aren't You Going to Taste It, Honey?" says it all. It shows the closeness I have felt with the readers and how, in one hour of an interview a friendship blooms, and, in many cases, continues for years. Often stories have taken me from campgrounds to palatial kitchens, to fields and orchards, and to church suppers and roadside markets, where the subject being interviewed has said, "Aren't you going to taste it, Honey?"

Yes, I wanted to taste the foods; the strawberries straight off the vine, a just-picked tomato, and a juicy peach pulled from the tree. I wanted to try a rib dripping with sauce from the grill, dip into the sauce made by a chef, and chomp on a pickle before a home canner tightened the lid. You must taste food to write about it, and indeed I have tasted my share in an ever-broadening career.

Our agriculturally fertile corner of America is equally fertile in food stories that seem to pop up as regularly as the corn sprouts through the earth and the apple blossoms promise a new crop.

An influx of immigrants—from eastern Europe in the late 1800s, from the Middle East in the 1920s, and from the Pacific rim recently— has made valuable contributions to the melting pot we are proud of. I have depended on them for stories, recipes, history, and a long list of friendships made.

Hopefully, the recipes and the comments that proceed each one will serve as a guide to take you with me on 41 glorious years of food reporting.

An important part of the reporting has been the photography. Photo shoots have changed over the years, as The Blade has added the technology to reproduce excellent color on the food page and pictures have become more integral to the stories.

Blade staff photographers have been a key in every production. Our food shots are the real thing. No foods were doctored to appear more perfect than they were. What readers have seen is exactly what I have cooked or baked, nothing more or less. In fact, when a pumpkin cheesecake came out of the oven with a crack down the center, the photographer asked if we shouldn't fill it with "Cool Whip, or just anything."

I said, "No, that's the way it should be printed so our readers will know we are not perfect." No patches. For years afterwards, calls came in from readers who wanted the recipe for the pumpkin cheesecake with the crack in it.

We have had a lot of fun shooting on location; cold soups at the polar bear pool at the Toledo Zoo, chili and cornbread in zero weather at a Metropark, Mud Hen Bars at Skeldon Stadium, and many picnics when the ants and bees arrived at the same time we did.

Cooking trends and appliances are traced in some of the recipe comments. Remember, 41 years ago microwave ovens were just an idea for the American home.

By 1980, the microwave was established as having the most impact on kitchen appliances since the refrigerator, but something else was making food news. "Whoosh!" was the headline on a food page article that read, "Enter the food processor, a dream machine. It may not be capable of doing everything in food preparation, but it doesn't take second place to any other."

Such innovations demanded recipes for their use. From the 50s to the mid-90s is a food trip from canned mushroom soup to tofu, sun-dried tomatoes, and chèvre. It takes us from an era of bread made the old-fashioned way, by instinct and feel, to machine-made bread that is pre-timed to mix, knead, rise, and bake automatically.

It takes us from the typical American post-war diet of jumbo slabs of beef to more healthful boneless, skinless chicken breasts fixed more ways than we care to remember. And it brings us to 1995, when we are safeguarding health by eating more vegetables, fruits, grains, and counting fat grams, although not forsaking high calorie desserts.

All of these trends, past and present, were considered in the selection of the 250 recipes. Decisions were difficult. Not all of my favorites made it to the book. It's like not being able to invite everyone you like to a party because there just isn't enough room.

Watching my life pass by on micro-fiche and old newspaper file copies to select recipes told me what I already knew. I've had a wonderful time being a food editor for a great newspaper in a rich agricultural and ethnic region of our country.

And, I would like to do it all over again.

Mary Alice Powell
January, 1995

Table of Contents

 Starters

Starters, those foods that literally are from soup to nuts, once were reserved as dinner first courses and party appetizers. In the 90's they are grazing foods with far-reaching importance in the new American eating mode.

Grazing was a tough sell to a food editor who spent a good deal of her childhood on her grandparents' farm and had the responsibility of "calling cows" after they had grazed all day in the pastures.

Now she can't think of a better way to define America's eating habits that are directed by time restraints and culinary adventure. Grazing is a way of modular dining that lets us eat what we want to, when it is most convenient.

According to grazing rules, it's OK to eat three different soups at one sitting or make a meal of several appetizers.

This diverse collection of Starters runs the gamut from time-honored Toledo recipes including Gracie's Sour Cream Potato Soup and Cabbage Soup to exciting new ones. The Ultimate Onion, White Chili, and Sun-Dried Tomato and Goat-Cheese Spread are newcomers. Our appreciation of ethnic foods is recognized in Lebanese Tabbouleh, Indian Masarie Dal, Greek Stuffed Grape Leaves, and others brought to our community from other lands.

On opposite page - Yellow peppers and carrots tint Chilled Sweet Pepper Soup (page 37) a lovely shade of orange. Mexican Cheesecake (page 28) is seasoned with cumin and chili powders.

Radishes with Sweet Butter and Caviar

Yields 48 appetizers

48 red radishes

1 cup unsalted butter, at room

    temperature and whipped

Caviar

Fresh dill sprigs

Sure, it's tedious to sculpt radishes into flowers and fill them with butter and caviar. But, think of the "ohs" and "ahs" that will come from guests. By the way, Ohio is the radish capital of the world.

Trim radish bottoms so they stand upright. Scoop out some of the top center portion of each radish and cut the top of the shell into a zigzag flower shape. Refrigerate in bowl of water for several hours to crisp. Drain radishes and pat dry. Spoon butter into a pastry bag fitted with a star tip, and pipe about 1 teaspoon butter into the center of each radish flower. Arrange radishes on a serving tray.

Spoon a little dab of caviar on top of the butter on each radish flower and garnish with sprig of dill.

Marinated Olives and Artichokes

Yields about 3 cups

1 (7 ¾-ounce) jar green olives

1 (5 ¾-ounce) can jumbo ripe olives

1 (8-ounce) jar marinated

　artichoke hearts

½ cup extra virgin olive oil

1 tablespoon finely minced fresh garlic

1 tablespoon balsamic vinegar

¼ teaspoon crushed red pepper flakes

Salt and freshly ground pepper to taste

Olive oil, balsamic vinegar, and red pepper flakes further enhance canned olives and artichoke hearts. Here is a relish to keep on hand in the refrigerator to serve with dinner or as an appetizer.

Drain olives. Combine olives and artichokes. Combine and add remaining ingredients. Stir to mix.

Cover and refrigerate overnight for flavors to mellow.

Mississippi Caviar

3 (16-ounce) cans black-eyed

    peas, drained

1 cup diced green pepper

3/4 cup diced onion, not sweet onion

3/4 cup diced jalapeño peppers,

    or less

2 ounces diced pimientos, drained

2 teaspoons minced garlic

1 cup Italian salad dressing

Salt

Red pepper sauce

When this recipe was tested before publication in 1991, the line up of ingredients seemed dull and uninteresting. But legumes were moving in fast as a trendy food, so we had to consider it. The completed dish was so good that the photographer took it home, and any food editor will tell you that doesn't happen very often.

Mix all ingredients and marinate, refrigerated, at least 3 days, but a week develops full flavor.

To serve, drain well and serve with tortilla chips, either cold or at room temperature.

Shrimp and Vegetables

Serves 6

1 cup fresh cauliflower florets

1 cup cherry tomatoes, pierced with a fork

1 cup small, whole, fresh mushrooms,

1 cup shrimp, cooked, shelled (½ pound)

1 cup sliced zucchini

¾ cup lemon juice

¾ cup vegetable oil

1 tablespoon chopped chives

2 teaspoons sugar

1 teaspoon salt

¼ teaspoon dill weed

5 drops hot pepper sauce

Only half a pound of shrimp? That's right, and it's plenty when there are so many good, fresh vegetables to select in the same appetizer assortment. Additional shrimp won't hurt.

Place vegetables and shrimp in shallow 1½-quart baking dish.
Combine other ingredients, and pour over vegetables and shrimp. Cover and refrigerate overnight.
Serve with toothpicks.

Spiced Baby Carrots

Serves 10 to 15

1 pound whole baby carrots

¾ cup vinegar

2 ½ cups water

⅔ cup sugar

2 tablespoons pickling spice

2 teaspoons salt

The convenience of the small sweet ready to eat carrots on the market was never more appreciated than they were during kitchen detail at a Mennonite work camp in Homestead, Florida, after Hurricane Andrew destroyed the city. "What can I do to help?" the Toledo food editor asked. "You can peel the carrots," she was told. Not one bunch, standard home size, but one bushel had to be prepared for the hungry church volunteers who were patching up Homestead homes.

Paring carrots has been a dreaded kitchen chore of the food editor since her mother assigned her the task at her rooming house in Adrian, Michigan; much too often, for too many relish trays. That's why she buys the small sweet carrots by the bagful and eats them like peanuts. Mother only said they were good for your eyes. She didn't know about beta carotene.

Scrub carrots and place in saucepan. Add all other ingredients. Bring to a boil slowly and cook 3 minutes on boil. Place carrots in bowl; add pickling solution to cover. Keep tightly covered in refrigerator.

Stuffed Snow Peas

1 ½ teaspoons horseradish

1 (3-ounce) package cream cheese

½ pound pea pods, blanched

½ pound smoked salmon, cut into strips

It took longer to arrange the photo set up for the colorful filled peapods than it did to make them. To lure readers to try the refreshing appetizer at poolside parties, we decided to place them on the end of a diving board. The setting was colorful; green peapods with a pink salmon garnish on a black platter and a blue pool beneath. But getting them to the end of the board came close to being a splashing success for the food editor, the photographer, and the peapods, which were the only things dressed for the pool party.

Whip horseradish into softened cream cheese and chill. Trim edge from each pea pod to open and pipe a small amount of cream cheese into each. Garnish with a strip of smoked salmon.

Tortilla Roll-Ups

2 (8-ounce) packages cream cheese,
   softened

2 tablespoons chopped green onion

1/2 cup chopped green, or black, olives

1/2 cup shredded Cheddar cheese

1/2 teaspoon garlic powder

8 medium flour tortillas

Slice filled and rolled tortillas to show off a mosaic pattern of green onion, olives, and Cheddar embedded in cream cheese. These freeze well.

Blend cream cheese until fluffy. Stir in onions, olives, cheese, and garlic powder. Spread in a thin layer on each tortilla, almost to the edges.

Tightly roll each tortilla and wrap individually in plastic wrap. Refrigerate several hours or overnight.

Slice into 1-inch, or larger, rounds and place flat on serving dish.

Wheel of an Appetizer Pie

Yields 8 to 10 servings

1 large round loaf of rye bread, cut
horizontally into 4 round slices

3 (8-ounce) packages cream cheese,
softened and tinted with V-8 juice

6, or more, hard-cooked eggs

2 large, or 3 small, cans tuna

Bottled slaw dressing

2 to 3 cans sardines, mashed with
lemon juice

Anchovy paste

Black caviar

Red caviar

Black and red caviar, egg salad, and cream cheese tinted pink form a rainbow of flavor and textures in this intriguing appetizer pie, credited to Doris Goldberg. Mrs. Goldberg is a poet whose verses were published in The Blade for many years.

Cut each of the 4 bread rounds into 8 wedges and re-form into a round on a serving plate. This makes it easier and neater to cut through the bread after the toppings are on. Kitchen shears work well to cut the bread.

Make egg salad by mashing the eggs with slaw dressing. Make tuna salad by mashing tuna with slaw dressing.

The toppings are arranged in concentric circles. The order of the circles of food are optional. Usually, the tinted cream cheese is spread around the outer edge, just inside are circles of egg salad, tuna salad, and mashed sardines. Anchovy paste and caviar form circles near the center.

Fresh Vegetable Pizza

2 (8-ounce) cans refrigerated
  crescent rolls

1 (8-ounce) carton dairy sour cream

1 to 2 tablespoons prepared
  horseradish

1/4 teaspoon salt

1/8 teaspoon pepper

1 teaspoon finely chopped onion

2 cups fresh mushrooms, chopped

1 cup chopped, seeded, tomatoes

1 cup small broccoli florets

1/2 cup chopped green pepper

1/2 cup chopped green onion

Guests who count fat grams at the cocktail party, or the summer picnic, need only add one gram for each piece of this fresh vegetable-topped pizza. The vegetables can be mixed and matched according to the availability. Just don't add any meat.

Separate dough into 4 long rectangles. Place rectangles crosswise in ungreased 15-by-10-inch baking pan. Press over bottom and 1 inch up sides to form crust. Seal perforations. Bake at 375 degrees for 14 to 19 minutes or until golden brown. Cool completely.

In small bowl, combine sour cream, horseradish, salt and pepper; blend until smooth. Spread evenly over cooled crust. Top with remaining ingredients. Cut into appetizer-sized pieces. Store in refrigerator.

Pizza By the Inch

Yields 12 to 14 appetizer portions

1 (1-pound) loaf French bread

1 (8-ounce) can pizza sauce

1 (1-pound) package frozen broccoli,

cauliflower, and carrots,

thawed and drained

1/2 cup sliced pepperoni, if desired

2 cups shredded mozzarella cheese

Vegetables outweigh meat in the thick topping on French bread. The ratio is one pound of vegetables to 2 ounces of pepperoni.

Slice bread in half lengthwise. Place, cut side up, on ungreased cookie sheet or broiler pan. Broil 4 to 6 inches from heat for 2 minutes until lightly browned. Remove from broiler.

Heat oven to 350 degrees. Spread pizza sauce over toasted bread. Arrange vegetables and pepperoni over sauce and sprinkle with cheese. Bake 20 minutes. Cut into appetizer-size portions.

Stuffed Grape Leaves

Yields 80

2 pounds ground chuck

2 cups long-grained rice, cooked

    and rinsed to remove starch

1 large dry onion, chopped

1 bunch green onions, chopped

2 sprigs parsley, chopped

1 tablespoon crumbled dried mint

1 tablespoon dry dill

1 teaspoon pepper

1/4 cup olive oil

1/4 cup lemon juice

80 preserved grape leaves

3 cups water

In autumn, women of Greek descent join in the age-old custom of gathering wild grape leaves to stuff. This recipe was written as the food editor watched Helen Arvantis of Toledo make stuffed grape leaves, or dolmas, with techniques she learned in her native country and with expertise developed by many years of practice.

Rinse grape leaves in boiling water and remove stems with scissors. Combine meat with rice, onions, parsley, dried mint, dill, pepper, and olive oil. Mix well. Spread out, 1 leaf at a time, on table or in palm of hand. Place 1 tablespoon of meat mixture near the stem end and turn the end of the leaf over the meat. Turn in sides of leaf as it is rolled, and always place the seam side down when it is completed.

If available, put lamb ribs in bottom of the cooking pan to add flavor and broth. Arrange stuffed grape leaves in cooking pan in layers and pour water over them. Place a plate snugly on top and cook over low to medium heat 20 minutes. Remove plate and add lemon juice.

Cover again and cook another 1 hour and 10 minutes. Add water as it is needed to keep rolls moist. If the leaves are small, or if some are broken, use two leaves for one roll.

The Ultimate Onion

Yields 4 to 6

3 cups cornstarch

1 ½ cups flour

2 teaspoons garlic salt

2 teaspoons paprika

1 teaspoon each: salt and pepper

24 ounces beer

4 to 6 onions, 4 inches in diameter
    or larger

Seasoned flour (below)

Creamy Chili Sauce (below)

Oil for frying

Pulling deep fried onion petals from the whole fried vegetable became the rage in national restaurant chains in the early 90s. Of course, home cooks wanted to try it, too, so we printed this popular version.

Mix cornstarch, flour, and seasonings until well blended. Add beer. Mix well. Cut about ¾ inch off top of onion; peel onion. Cut 12 to 16 vertical wedges into onion, but do not cut through the bottom, which is the root end. Remove about 1 inch of "petals" from center of onion.

Dip cut onion into seasoned flour and remove excess by shaking. Then dip into batter and remove excess by gently shaking the onion. Separate petals to coat thoroughly with batter. Mix batter again after standing, to blend ingredients.

Gently place prepared onion in fryer basket in hot oil and deep-fry at 375 to 400 degrees 1½ minutes. Turn over and fry another 1 to 1½ minutes longer, or until golden brown. Drain on paper towels.

Place onion upright in shallow bowl and remove center core with circular cutter or apple corer. Serve hot with dipping sauce, placed in the center.

SEASONED FLOUR: Combine 2 cups flour, 4 teaspoons paprika, 2 teaspoons garlic powder, ½ teaspoon pepper, and ¼ teaspoon ground red pepper. Mix well.
CREAMY CHILI SAUCE: Combine 1 pint mayonnaise, 1 pint sour cream, ½ cup chili sauce, and ½ teaspoon ground red pepper. Mix well.

Old-Fashioned Lemonade

Yields enough for about 36 glasses

6 lemons, juiced

3 lemons, rind grated

4 cups sugar

4 cups water

Lemonade made from homemade syrup is as nostalgic as picking an apple in the orchard and sitting under a tree to eat it or walking down a lane on a summer day swinging a picnic basket.

Combine the juice of 6 lemons with the grated rind of 3 lemons. Chill mixture overnight. In a saucepan, bring sugar and water to a rolling boil, and boil gently for 5 minutes. Let syrup cool, and strain the lemon mixture into it. Store in refrigerator in a glass container until needed.

To use, put 2 generous tablespoons of syrup into a glass half filled with cracked ice and stir in enough cold water to fill the glass.

Pseudo Champagne Punch

1 (12-ounce) can frozen white grape juice

1 (16-ounce) can frozen lemonade

3 (1-liter) bottles club soda

Decades before non-alcoholic wines were on the market, this non-alcoholic beverage became the hallmark of Toledo Museum of Art receptions. Bubbles are included.

Combine all ingredients. For museum parties, the punch is poured over an ice ring made with whole strawberries and lemon slices.

Apple Dippers

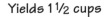

1 (8-ounce) package cream cheese,

    softened

3 to 4 tablespoons apple juice

    or cider

½ cup grated apples

2 teaspoons chopped chives

Dash salt

Ohio apples are a valued commodity. Here, they are shredded and added to a dip. The dippers? Fresh, crisp apple slices, celery sticks, or whole-grain crackers.

Combine cream cheese and apple juice until smooth and creamy. Blend in grated apples. Stir in chives and salt. Chill.

Serve with celery sticks and apple wedges, or another fresh fruit such as pears, cut into wedges.

Beer Cheese

1 ¼ pounds extra-sharp Cheddar cheese

2 garlic cloves, minced

1 (7-ounce) bottle beer

⅛ teaspoon salt

Hot pepper sauce

This is a hearty, easy recipe with plenty of garlic and a bottle of beer. Only five ingredients make a big batch. It keeps well in the refrigerator, but it is thoughtful to pack half of the batch in an attractive crock to give to a friend.

Grate cheese and add garlic. Add beer, salt, and hot pepper sauce; mix to blend well. It will be soft, but will harden in the refrigerator. It should be made in advance. Serve with crackers and celery sticks.

Bleu Cheesecake

2 (8-ounce) package cream cheese

2 cups crumbled bleu cheese

1 cup sour cream

1/8 teaspoon white pepper

3 eggs

1¼ cups sour cream

Red peppers or whole pimientos

Green onion tops

Here is a great addition to the buffet party table. Watch the bleu cheese lovers. They'll clean the plate!

Beat cream and bleu cheeses in large mixing bowl until light and fluffy, about 5 minutes. Mix in 1 cup sour cream and pepper. Add eggs, 1 at a time, mixing well after each addition.

Pour mixture into buttered 9-inch springform pan. Bake in 300-degree oven about an hour until wooden pick comes out clean. Remove from oven and let stand 5 minutes.

Carefully spread 1¼ cups sour cream over top. Return to oven 5 minutes. Cool completely on wire rack. Garnish with peppers and onion tops.

Bread Basket Spinach Dip

Serves 10

1 large round loaf of bread

1 (8-ounce) carton sour cream

1 package frozen, chopped spinach,

    drained

1 package dry vegetable soup mix

1 cup mayonnaise

1 (8-ounce) can sliced water chestnuts

The idea of converting hollowed bread into an edible bowl for spinach dip has been around for years. Our dip is crunchy with water chestnuts. The bowl is attractive, and guests seem to enjoy it. Be a leader and tear into the bowl yourself when the bread cubes are gone. Otherwise, no one else will start it, and you will be left with a soggy bread shell.

Remove top of bread and hollow out to leave a 2-inch shell. Cut remaining bread into cubes and toast in 300-degree oven. Combine other ingredients and spoon dip into hollowed bread. Serve encircled with bread cubes.

Broccamole

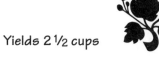

2 cups broccoli pieces

¼ cup sour cream

2 tablespoons finely minced onion

1 tablespoon mayonnaise

2 tablespoons lemon juice

¼ teaspoon curry powder

This is one to make when the avocados are as hard as rocks and won't ripen in a paper bag, even if the avocado growers say they will. Broccoli comes to the rescue in this dip with a touch of curry.

Cook broccoli until very tender in boiling, salted water. Drain well and cool. Add sour cream, onion, mayonnaise, lemon juice, and curry powder to blender or food processor. Mix several seconds.

Add broccoli. Cover and blend to purée, but stop several times to scrape sides. Chill several hours before serving in a bowl, encircled by fresh vegetables.

Chicken Liver Paté

Yields 2 cups

1 small onion, peeled and quartered

½ cup butter

1 pound chicken livers

¼ cup heavy cream

Salt and pepper

2 tablespoons dry sherry

Parsley

In the late 70s, food processors received the nod of approval as a portable appliance that was here to stay, and recipes from breads to patés proved its versatility.

Using steel blade, chop onion in food processor. Melt butter in skillet and add chopped onion and chicken livers. Sauté over medium heat until just cooked, about 5 minutes.

Cool slightly. Process livers, cream, salt, pepper, and sherry. Blend well. Pack into bowl and chill about 4 hours before serving with parsley garnish.

24

Cream Cheese and Chutney

1 (8-ounce) package cream cheese

1 (9-ounce) jar chutney

There are several kinds of chutney in the marketplace—spicy hot, mellow, and sweet. Choose a couple to have on hand for this quick appetizer.

Place cream cheese block in center of serving dish. Pour and evenly distribute chutney over it. Serve with crackers.

Masarie Dal

1 small onion, diced

2 tablespoons vegetable oil

2 cups dry red lentils, washed

1¼ teaspoons salt

1 large clove garlic, minced

¼ teaspoon cumin seeds

To enhance the experience of eating dal, an Indian dip that is made of lentils and is heavy with garlic and spiced with cumin seeds, it is nice to eat poori. Poori is Indian deep-fried bread, and a recipe for it is included in the bread section of this book.

Sauté onion in oil in 3-quart Dutch oven. Set aside 3 to 5 minutes to cool. Add 4 cups water, washed lentils, and salt to fried onion. Bring to a boil over medium heat and cook until lentils turn pale yellow and are the consistency of thick gravy. Set aside.

Sauté garlic in 2 tablespoons vegetable oil in small frying pan over high heat until golden brown. Pour garlic and oil over cooked lentils. Sprinkle with cumin seeds.

Green Pea Guacamole

3 cups green peas, fresh or frozen

2 tablespoons lemon juice

1 cup red onions

2 teaspoons minced garlic

1 teaspoon ground cumin

¼ teaspoon freshly ground black
   pepper

⅛ teaspoon ground red pepper

When Dr. Dean Ornish proclaimed to Americans that a diet of only 10 per cent fat would be a deterrent to heart disease, low-fat recipes were developed by adventurous chefs. Green pea guacamole, which is far better in flavor than it sounds, is a substitute for the dip made with oil-laden avocados that Dr. Ornish warns against. The color is as green as a shamrock, and one-quarter cup has only 0.3 fat grams!

If fresh peas are used, steam them just until tender; only thaw frozen peas, to preserve the fresh green color.

Purée peas in blender or food processor with lemon juice, onions, garlic, cumin, and black pepper. Add ground red pepper and salt to taste.

Kahlua Dip

1 pint sour cream

4 tablespoons brown sugar

4 tablespoons Kahlua liqueur

This incredible three-ingredient dip surfaced in 1980 as the cocktail party recipe of the year and an ideal way to present fresh strawberries and fruits.   In the 90s it's equally popular, but hosts are substituting yogurt for the sour cream. Is it as good? It's a trade-off.

Combine all ingredients and let stand at least half an hour. Serve in a bowl encircled by whole strawberries, fresh pineapple spears, bing cherries, peaches, or other fresh fruit.

Mexican Cheesecake

Yields 15-20 servings

1 cup finely ground corn tortilla chips

2 tablespoons unsalted butter, melted

4 tablespoons flour

1 pound light cream cheese

2 cups low-fat yogurt cheese (below)

4 large eggs

1 teaspoon dried oregano

1 ½ teaspoons cumin powder

½ teaspoon garlic powder

1 teaspoon chili powder

½ teaspoon freshly ground black pepper

¼ teaspoon each: ground red pepper
    and salt

Salsa, homemade or commercial

From the thousands of recipes Betty Rosbottom has demonstrated at LaBelle Pomme Cooking School in Columbus, she circles this southwestern appetizer cake as her favorite. The highly seasoned appetizer bakes on a tortilla chip crust in a springform pan. A lesson in how to make yogurt cheese is a bonus.

Spray 9-inch springform pan with nonstick vegetable cooking spray. Combine ground tortilla chips, melted butter, and flour. Mix well and pat onto bottom of pan. Bake in 350-degree oven about 10 minutes to set, remove, but do not turn oven off.

Beat cream cheese and yogurt cheese with electric mixer until smooth, about 2 minutes. Add eggs, 1 at a time, and mix to blend. Add seasonings and mix 1 to 2 minutes more.

Pour filling into prepared pan; spread evenly with a spatula. Bake on center rack until firm, 35 to 40 minutes. Remove from oven and cool completely. Cover and refrigerate.

To serve, remove sides from springform pan and place cheesecake on serving tray. Spread salsa over the top of the cheesecake and place more in serving bowl. Garnish with tortilla chips.

LOW FAT YOGURT CHEESE: Make cheese from low-fat yogurt by placing 4 cups of plain yogurt in fine mesh sieve over a bowl and refrigerating for at least 12 hours. The water, almost half the amount of yogurt, will drain off, leaving a solid mass of yogurt cheese. The cheese can be refrigerated up to 2 days.

Photo on page 2

Mexican-Style Layered Dip

Yields 12 to 15 appetizer servings

3 ½ cups drained, cooked or canned

    pinto, kidney, or pink beans

¼ cup chopped onion

2 tablespoons oil

1 package taco seasoning mix

¼ cup water

1 cup dairy sour cream, divided

Guacamole

Tomato salsa (see below)

1 cup shredded Cheddar cheese

Tortilla chips

This layered dip is like the long-lost relative who always shows up for parties. Guests may say, when they spot the dip made of beans, sour cream, guacamole, salsa, and Cheddar cheese, "Not that again." Then they dip a tortilla chip in deep to dredge up all that they can.

Mash half of the beans. Sauté onion in oil. Add mashed beans, taco seasoning mix, and water. Cook and stir 5 minutes. Stir in ¼ cup sour cream and whole beans; cool.

Spread bean mixture on a large platter. Top with layers of guacamole, tomato salsa, remaining ¾ cup sour cream, and cheese so that each layer is smaller than the one below it. Garnish with tortilla chips and serve with more chips for dipping.

TOMATO SALSA: Combine 2 diced tomatoes; 1 small can ripe olives, drained and chopped; 1 (4-ounce) can green chilies, drained and chopped; and ½ cup sliced green onions. Makes about 2½ cups.

Pesto Cheese with Sun-Dried Tomatoes

Yields 12 servings

1 garlic clove

1 cup fresh basil leaves

3 teaspoons extra virgin olive oil

7 tablespoons Parmesan cheese

12 sun-dried tomatoes, rehydrated
according to package
directions and drained

¼ cup low-fat cream cheese at room
temperature

Just when you think nothing new can come down the food pike, along comes something wonderful like sun-dried tomatoes. Tomatoes and basil are perfect partners. One of the best ways to enjoy basil leaves is in a pesto. They are here, teamed in a dashing appetizer that turns out to be red, white, and green layers. Isn't that Italian?

In food processor, mince garlic. Scrape down sides of bowl. Add basil leaves, olive oil, and 3 tablespoons Parmesan cheese. Process until finely chopped.

Spoon into small glass bowl. Process tomatoes and remaining oil. Spread tomatoes on top of pesto. Mix cream cheese and remaining Parmesan.

Carefully spread cream cheese mixture over tomatoes. Serve with thin slices of fresh French bread or crackers.

Rosalynn Carter's Cheese Ring

Serves 8

1 pound grated sharp Cheddar cheese

1 cup chopped peanuts

1 cup mayonnaise

1 small onion, grated

Black pepper

Dash ground red pepper

Early during a First Lady's term in the White House, she learns that her recipes are in demand from every organization in the United States that is publishing a cookbook. It is common for one recipe to be selected to answer all requests. This is the one Rosalynn Carter chose to represent the Carter administration from coast to coast. It is no shock that peanuts are an ingredient, but it was a surprise that the cheese ring was served, complete with the strawberry jam center, when the food editor had lunch with Mrs. Carter in the White House.

Mold all ingredients with hands into desired shape. Chill in refrigerator. When ready to serve, fill center with strawberry preserves, or use as a spread without preserves.

Seafood Spread

Serves 6 to 8

1 (8-ounce) package cream cheese
   at room temperature

1 (8-ounce) bottle chili sauce

1 can crab or shrimp

This 1987 recipe calls for chili sauce, but in the 90s the appropriate substitute is salsa, hot and spicy.

Spread cream cheese over serving plate. Top with chili sauce; sprinkle with crab or shrimp. Serve with crackers.

Bagna Cauda

½ cup butter

½ cup olive oil

3 garlic cloves, mashed

1 can flat anchovies with oil, mashed

Freshly ground black pepper

We have the Italians to thank for this simple, but dynamite, dip. Even people who avoid anchovies because of their high salt content soon learn they are diffused here by the bland vegetable dippers. Sliced turnips and jicama are particularly compatible with bagna cauda.

Combine all ingredients in saucepan; simmer 5 minutes. Serve hot with raw, fresh vegetables.

Vegetable Cheese Spread

Yields ¾ cup

½ cup whipped cream cheese

2 tablespoons each: minced celery,

    green onion, red bell pepper,

    and carrot

1 tablespoon chopped fresh dill

Lynn Redgrave, the energetic English beauty and theatrical star, is just like the rest of us when it comes to the 4 p.m. slump. "This is one of my standbys about 4 o'clock in the afternoon of a heavy work day, when lunch is long past and dinner seems far away. I like to spread a little on a rice cake or two," Ms. Redgrave said in an interview when she shared this recipe.

Process cream cheese until fluffy and stir in remaining ingredients. Cover and refrigerate to blend flavors, at least 30 minutes.

Each tablespoon is 34 calories and 3 grams of fat.

Raspberry Brie in Phyllo

Serves 12 to 16

½ (1-pound) package phyllo dough

½ pound butter, melted

1 ¼ cup raspberry preserves

1 (2-pound) wheel Brie

Thin slices of French baguette

A winning candidate for grazing dinner parties, this colorful appetizer is from Chuck Welker, chef at Nazareth Hall, Grand Rapids, Ohio, and whose family was in the catering business in Defiance, Ohio, for a long time. The surprise in the phyllo encased Brie is raspberry preserves, which ooze out when the dough is cut.

Place 1 sheet of phyllo on work table and brush with butter. Place another phyllo on top and brush with butter. Repeat until there are 6 layers of phyllo, each brushed with butter. Make a second stack with 6 layers.

Generously coat top of Brie wheel with raspberry preserves. Place cheese in center of one stack of phyllo. Bring the edges of the dough up around the cheese. Place the second stack on top of the Brie. The top and the bottom layers of phyllo will seal together as it is baked.

If desired, fold a single sheet of phyllo into a flower-like design and place it in the center of the wrapped Brie.

Bake 20 minutes in 350-degree oven. Encircle with small, thin French bread slices and serve immediately so that the cheese is melted.

Reuben Dip

1 (8-ounce) package cream cheese

½ cup sour cream

1 (2½-ounce) package corned beef, or

    chipped beef, diced well

½ cup sauerkraut

1 cup finely shredded Swiss cheese

¼ teaspoon Worcestershire sauce

¼ cup milk

License is taken with the Reuben sandwich to make a hot dip that is served with rye bread rounds. Dust off the chafing dish and serve it in grand style.

Combine all ingredients in saucepan and heat over low heat. Serve warm with rye bread rounds, crackers, and celery sticks.

Chilled Sweet Pepper Soup

Serves 4

---

1 tablespoon butter

2 medium carrots, sliced

1 large onion, sliced

1 yellow pepper, sliced

1 (10-ounce) can chicken broth

1 (3-ounce) package cream cheese

Dash ground red pepper

½ cup light cream or milk

Purple, yellow, red, orange, and green—the rainbow of colors in sweet pepper displays in supermarket produce departments is mind-boggling. And to think we lived so long with only green peppers and an occasional red one. The colorful new peppers are so attractive it's fun to buy some of each color to make a basket arrangement for the kitchen table. This cold soup recipe, which made the rounds through Toledo neighborhoods in the summer of 1994, calls on a yellow pepper, which, with carrots, makes a lovely shade of light orange. Sure, it can be eaten hot, but try it chilled the first time around.

Melt butter. Add carrots, onion, and yellow pepper. Sauté until onion is transparent. Add chicken broth and cook until vegetables are tender. Cool slightly.

Purée in blender or food processor. Add cream cheese and blend. Add red pepper to taste. Blend in light cream or milk.

photo page 2

Blender Gazpacho

3 cups tomato juice

2 tablespoons salad oil

2 tablespoons wine vinegar

1 garlic clove

2 medium tomatoes, pared and
    quartered

1 small cucumber, pared and
    cut into pieces

1 small green pepper, cut into pieces

3 celery ribs, cut into pieces

1/4 cup onion, cut into pieces

4 parsley sprigs

2 slices bread, torn into pieces

1 teaspoon salt

Freshly ground pepper

1 cup croutons

Cucumber slices

Gazpacho should be the official Toledo dish. This cold salad soup is the national dish of Spain, and Toledo, Spain, is our sister city with which we enjoy student and cultural exchange programs. Besides, the best tomatoes anywhere, any year, are grown in Ohio.

Put tomato juice, salad oil, wine vinegar, and garlic in blender or food processor and blend until garlic is minced.

Add tomato, cucumber, green pepper, celery, onion, parsley, bread, and salt and pepper. Blend until vegetables are puréed. Pour into a 2-quart container. Cover and chill well.

Serve from bowl or in cups, topped with croutons and sliced cucumbers. For added texture and color interest, pass chopped green pepper, onion, cucumber, and hard-cooked eggs for garnish.

Cabbage Soup

Yields 10 generous servings

---

2 (1-pound) solid heads cabbage

2 quarts beef stock

2 tablespoons butter

1½ cups coarsely chopped onion

1 cup finely chopped carrots

2 cups celery root, scraped and cut into
    fine strips, or substitute chopped celery

1 teaspoon salt, if desired

1 bay leaf, broken

1 teaspoon dill weed

1 pound garlic sausage or kielbasa, cut
    diagonally into ¼-inch slices

2 tablespoons minced parsley

2 cups tomatoes, peeled, seeded,
    and chopped

2 cups diced potatoes

Freshly ground black pepper

Sour cream for garnish

Count the good-for-you ingredients in a hearty soup, typical of midwestern winter fare. If you found seven vegetables you were right; then add kielbasa, seasonings, and dollops of sour cream for garnish.

Slice cabbage into quarter wedges. Remove cores and any hard ribs. Coarsely chop cabbage and put aside. Pour stock into 6-quart pot or kettle and bring to a simmer while preparing the vegetables.

In a large skillet, melt butter until it bubbles and add onions, carrots, and celery root. Cover and cook for 10 minutes over medium-low heat until the vegetables are translucent and almost tender. Turn contents of skillet into stock pot and add salt, bay leaf, and dill weed. Simmer.

Lightly sauté sausage pieces in the same skillet until they are slightly brown and the fat is released. Drain meat and discard fat. Add sausage, parsley, tomatoes, and potatoes to the soup. Continue to simmer for an additional 20 minutes for a total of 40 minutes.

Serve hot, seasoned with freshly ground pepper. Sour cream can be stirred into the soup, Russian style, if desired.

Columbian's Black Bean Soup

1 pound dry black beans

3 quarts water

Olive oil

3 onions, chopped

2 green peppers, cut into strips

5 garlic cloves

2 bay leaves

1 teaspoon oregano

2 teaspoons salt

1/2 teaspoon pepper

White rice

Additional chopped onions

Additional olive oil

Red wine vinegar

Newspaper food editors are among those who head for the Columbian Restaurant in Ybor City, Florida, for a bowl of black bean soup, made from this recipe. Add crunchy hot bread, and lunch is served.

Rinse beans and soak overnight in water. The next day, boil the beans in fresh water. In a small amount of olive oil, sauté onions and green peppers until limp but not brown. Add garlic, bay leaves, oregano, salt and pepper. Cook 5 minutes and add to black beans.

Cook until beans are very tender. If desired, serve over white rice and top with chopped onions. Pass olive oil and red wine vinegar in cruets to dribble over individual servings.

Crouton-Cheese-Topped Onion Soup

Serves 6

¼ cup butter

4 cups sliced onions (2 large)

1 to 2 tablespoons sugar

2 tablespoons flour

6 bouillon cubes, smashed, and added to

6 cups water, or 6 cups of beef stock

1 teaspoon salt

Pepper to taste

1 tablespoon butter

2 additional sliced onions

Half-inch slices French bread, toasted

Grated Gruyere cheese

Grated Parmesan cheese

Crisp caramelized onions add an intense, robust flavor to the soup pot. An introduction of sherry gives a special touch to this version of a classic soup.

Melt butter in large saucepan and add sliced onions. Use more onions, if desired, for a thicker soup. Cover and simmer on low heat for 30 minutes. Add sugar and flour, and stir-cook a few minutes; add bouillon cubes and water, or beef stock. For a nice wine flavor, cooking sherry can be used for part of the water or stock. Season with salt and pepper. Cover and simmer another 30 minutes.

In some recipes, rather than simmering the onions in butter as is done here, it is recommended that the onions be sautéed to a golden brown. Here it is recommended that the two additional onions be caramelized in the additional portion of butter until they are browned and crisp and then added, with the drippings, to the onion-soup pot for color and extra taste.

Fill individual earthenware bowls with the soup and top each with the toasted French bread. Let bread sink into the soup somewhat before covering generously with Gruyere cheese; sprinkle with Parmesan cheese. Broil until cheese is bubbly. Parmesan is easily burned under the broiler.

Gracie's Sour Cream Potato Soup

Yields 4 quarts

12 slices bacon, cut in small,

 even squares

12 or more leeks or green onions,

 chopped

1/2 cup yellow onions, chopped

1/4 cup flour

8 cups beef or chicken broth

5 pounds potatoes, pared and cubed

4 egg yolks

2 cups sour cream

2 tablespoons minced parsley

2 teaspoons chervil

Each year, former members of the Urban Athletic Club call and ask for a "Gracie recipe." This potato soup recipe is one of the few that was shared by Gracie Shutt, the gracious lady who operated a private club in the basement of her home on Lincoln Avenue. She was known for colossal hamburgers served on white bread, and there was always soup to go with them. Friends remember well how she laboriously cut the bacon for the potato soup by hand into identical squares, even after they gave her a food processor.

Sauté bacon until crisp; add leeks or green onions and yellow onions to bacon and drippings. Sift flour into skillet and cook until thickened. Slowly stir in broth.

Add potatoes and cook until soft, not mushy. Combine sour cream and egg yolks. Add a little of the soup mixture to the sour cream and yolk mixture and then add all to soup pot. Otherwise, the sour cream will curdle.

Add parsley and chervil 5 minutes before serving. If the soup is made in advance, add the sour cream and egg yolks when it is heated before serving.

Kerr House Lettuce Soup

Serves 6

2 medium carrots

3 large leeks

3 tablespoons safflower oil

2 medium heads romaine, torn into
   small pieces

4 cups chicken broth

Grated Cheddar cheese

Clients who visit the Kerr House in Grand Rapids, Ohio, go home with the recipe for this low-fat, low-calorie soup. The Kerr House, a Victorian mansion furnished with antiques, is a health and fitness center with a national reputation.

Clean carrots with vegetable brush, remove ends; chop carrots. Slice white portion of leeks. Heat oil in large, heavy skillet. Add leeks; sauté on low heat 5 minutes. Push to one side of skillet. Add carrots to other side of pan and continue to simmer for 15 minutes. Remove carrots; add romaine and simmer about 10 minutes.

In a blender or food processor, purée carrots with half the chicken broth. Set aside. Purée leeks and romaine in remaining chicken broth, being sure as much oil as possible is removed from them and the pan. Combine the puréed mixtures and return to pan to heat for about 15 minutes. Serve hot, garnished with Cheddar cheese.

Low Calorie Vegetable Soup

1 large head cabbage

6 large onions

2 green peppers

2 large cans stewed, or diced,

    tomatoes

½ bunch celery

1 to 2 pounds carrots

Dry onion soup mix, to taste

Who needs meat when you can make such a flavorful soup without it? The onion soup mix gives ample seasoning, and you can mix and match vegetables according to what's in the crisper and the best buys in the supermarket.

Clean and cut vegetables into medium pieces. Cover with water and boil until vegetables are tender. Season with dry onion soup mix. For variation, add turnips, green beans, and/or cauliflower.

Oysters Rockefeller Soup

Serves 6

1 (10-ounce) box frozen, chopped spinach, thawed

1 small onion

2 green onions

2 celery ribs with leaves

1/4 cup parsley

1/2 cup iceberg lettuce

2 tablespoons butter

2 tablespoons anchovy paste

1 teaspoon seasoned salt

1/4 teaspoon pepper

Juice of 1/2 lemon

2 tablespoons flour

2 dozen small to medium oysters and liquid

1 (10 3/4-ounce) can condensed chicken broth

2 teaspoons Worcestershire sauce, or more

1 1/2 cups half and half

2 tablespoons each: Parmesan cheese and seasoned bread crumbs

All the Rockefeller ingredients are here—spinach, parsley, anchovies, and oysters, but this time they are combined into a soup. No shells!

Squeeze spinach dry and puree with onion, green onion, celery, parsley, and lettuce in a food processor. Melt butter and add puréed vegetables. Sauté 8 minutes over medium heat and stir. Stir in anchovy paste, salt, pepper, and lemon juice. Stir in flour. Gently add oysters and their liquid. Simmer about 3 minutes.

Gradually add chicken broth and Worcestershire sauce. Bring to a boil. Turn down heat and simmer 5 more minutes. Add half and half, Parmesan cheese, and bread crumbs; simmer another 10 minutes.

In New Orleans, Herbsaint liquor is added to the soup just before it is served. Or you can add more Worcestershire sauce. The recipe can be made a day in advance up to the point of adding the oysters, but it cannot be frozen and should not be kept more than 1 day.

Salmon Chowder

1 (15-ounce) can salmon, preferably red

2 tablespoons butter

1 small onion, chopped

2 celery ribs, diced

2 (10½ -ounce) can cream of celery soup

2 soup cans milk

1 (12-ounce) can cream-style corn

1 (12-ounce) can whole kernel corn

1 tablespoon dill weed

Keep an open mind when you see all of the canned products in this recipe. It's a winner. Trust the food editor, who made it for a friend recovering from surgery. She was almost like new the next day.

Remove skin and center bone from salmon. Sauté onion and celery in butter until soft. Add remaining ingredients and heat soup. Do not boil.

Squash Sage Soup

Serves 8

1 (14½-ounce) can chicken broth

2 small or 1 large butternut squash,
   about 1½ pounds

1 medium onion, chopped

1 tart apple, peeled and chopped

¼ cup chopped fresh parsley

3 teaspoons minced fresh sage leaves,
   divided

Salt and white pepper

1 cup milk

Additional fresh sage leaves for garnish

It was early October when three food editor's friends from Nashville, Memphis, and Salt Lake City came to Toledo for a weekend visit. What to serve was challenging. This seasonal squash soup, punctuated with fresh sage, was the perfect choice to ward off Murphy's Law. For the record, the main dish was Chicken Parmesan Rolls made from the recipe in Main Dishes.

Combine broth, squash, onion, apple, and parsley and 2 teaspoons sage in 2-quart saucepan. Heat to boiling; reduce heat to low. Cover and simmer 30 minutes until vegetables are tender. Blend squash mixture smooth in blender or food processor. Season with salt and white pepper.

Return to saucepan. Add milk and more salt and pepper, if desired. Add remaining 1 teaspoon sage. Simmer 4 minutes over medium heat.

Garnish soup tureen or each serving with fresh sage. Because moisture content in squash varies, it may be necessary to thin soup with additional milk and adjust seasoning.

This soup will keep, covered, up to 3 days in the refrigerator.

Steak and Mushroom Soup

Serves 8 to 10

Marinade:

2/3 cup oil

2 tablespoons each: lemon juice
    and soy sauce

1 tablespoon each: dark brown sugar
    and Dijon mustard

1 large garlic clove, minced

1¼ pounds steak, trimmed and
    cut into 1-inch strips

Soup:

3 tablespoons each: olive oil and butter

2 small carrots, scraped and
    finely chopped

2 small celery ribs, finely chopped

3 medium onions,
    ½ coarsely chopped, ½ sliced

1 pound mushrooms, thickly sliced

Flour for dusting

5 cups beef broth, or more

1 large bay leaf

1½ teaspoons salt, or less

¼ teaspoon freshly ground pepper

1¼ pounds escarole, washed and torn into
    bite-sized pieces, with stems broken

Steak strips marinated in a mustard-soy sauce and handfuls of escarole put this hearty, savory mixture at the head of the line as a main-dish soup. Lee Bailey, a New England cookbook author, gets the credit for creating it.

Whisk marinade ingredients in medium bowl and add steak, being sure all is submerged. Set aside 1 hour or refrigerate overnight, covered.

Heat half the olive oil and butter in large stockpot. Add carrot, celery, and chopped onion. Cook over medium to high heat until golden, about 5 minutes.

Add mushrooms and continue cooking until just wilted. Remove and set aside. Add remaining oil and butter to the pot. Pat steak dry and flour, shaking off excess. Brown in oil and butter over medium heat. Do not allow flour to burn. Remove and set aside.

Return vegetables and mushrooms to pot; add sliced onions. Add 5 cups beef broth. Bring to a simmer and add bay leaf, salt, and pepper. Simmer 15 minutes.

Add steak and simmer another 10 minutes before adding escarole. You may want to add more stock here if the soup is too thick. Simmer only long enough for escarole to become tender.

Cream of Parisian Vegetable Soup

Serves 6

16 to 18 ounces frozen vegetables

    (cauliflower, broccoli, and carrots)

2 cups water

½ cup butter

½ cup margarine

½ cup chopped celery

½ cup chopped onion

1 cup flour

4 chicken bouillon cubes

6 cups cold milk

1 cup diced, cooked ham

1 teaspoon white pepper

Mastering the basic technique of cream soups opens a fascinating category in cooking creativity. There is no limit to the kinds of soups that can be made, from asparagus to zucchini, and including lush seafood combinations. Cream soups also are excellent depositories for leftovers— a little broccoli, a couple of carrots, an onion that is beginning to dry up, a smidgen of ham. Within weeks you will want to purchase a soup pot to make it official. Only homemade soups will be served at your house.

Cook vegetables in water until tender; drain.

Melt butter and margarine; sauté onions and celery until the onions are translucent. Add flour and stir to blend. Crush and add chicken bouillon cubes.

Stir in cold milk and stir until thick and smooth. Add vegetables. Add ham and season with white pepper and salt.

White Chili

1 pound great northern beans

2 pound boneless chicken breasts

1 tablespoon olive oil

2 medium onions, chopped

4 garlic cloves, minced

2 (4-ounce) cans chopped
    mild green chilies

2 teaspoons ground cumin

1½ teaspoons dried oregano,
    crumbled

¼ teaspoon ground cloves

¼ teaspoon ground red pepper

5 cups canned chicken broth

1 (7-ounce) bottle beer

Optional:

½ teaspoon each: white, lemon,
    and black pepper

3 cups grated Monterey Jack cheese

Sour cream and salsa

Chili-heads, those guys who live for a bowl of red, keep their recipes a secret and wear outlandish clothes when they enter chili contests, probably don't have much to do with even the name White Chili, let alone the taste it. But for the rest of the world, it has been a real "'Wow!" since it arrived on the chili scene five years ago. White beans, chicken breast, and broth keep the name honest.

Cover beans with water and soak overnight. Drain. Place chicken in large saucepan. Add cold water to cover and bring to a simmer. Cook until just tender, about 15 minutes. Drain and cool. Remove skin; cut into small pieces.

Drain beans. In same pot, sauté onions in oil until they are translucent; stir in garlic, chilies, cumin, oregano, cloves, and ground red pepper; sauté 2 minutes. Add beans, broth, and beer. If desired, stir in optional peppers. Bring to a boil; reduce heat and simmer until beans are very tender, about 2 hours. Stir occasionally.

Add chicken and 1 cup cheese; stir until cheese melts. Season with salt to taste. Serve with remaining cheese, sour cream, and salsa for guests to spoon onto chili if they wish.

Wild Rice Soup

1 large onion, diced

5 large, fresh mushrooms, diced,

    or 1 small can sliced mushrooms, drained

1/3 cup butter

1 cup flour

8 cups hot chicken broth

2 cups cooked wild rice

1 cup half and half

Salt and pepper

2 tablespoons sherry or dry white wine

Wild rice and mushrooms are combined in a delectable soup that's straight from where the rice is grown, Minnesota.

Sauté onion and mushrooms in butter about 3 minutes or just until vegetables are soft. Stir in flour. Cook and stir until flour is mixed in, but do not let it begin to brown.

Slowly add hot chicken broth and stir until the vegetable and flour mixture is blended well. Add cooked rice and half and half. Season with salt and pepper. Heat thoroughly, stirring often. Add sherry or wine and heat gently, but do not boil.

The soup can be prepared to the point of adding half and half and set aside until needed. Reheat and continue with recipe.

Main Dishes

The Main Dish anchors the menu. Once chicken, beef, pork, turkey, fish, or no meat at all has been chosen according to budget, health, and taste preferences, the rest of the menu falls into place.

Since Americans have turned to smaller portions as a safeguard to health, Main Dishes yield more servings than they once did. No longer is it nutritionally correct to plan on a half-pound, or more, of meat, per serving.

Such restriction is not easily followed when Tony Packo's Stuffed Cabbage Rolls, from Toledo's famous Hungarian café; Crab-Stuffed Walleye, featuring Lake Erie fish; or Best Meat Loaf, from a meat loaf recipe contest, are served.

To those treasured Toledo Main Dishes on the following pages, add other favorites: Woody's Barbecue Sauce, seasoned with memories; an elegant Pork Loin Stuffed with Apples and Prunes, which the food editor serves often. Chicken appears in several dishes, plain and fancy, from quickly made Lemon Cutlets to a baked version with Yorkshire Pudding.

Our Main Dishes go all the way to Z for zucchini. Remember old Zucchini Impossible Pie? It's here.

Opposite Page: Spooning deep inside Dinner in a Pumpkin (page 45) yields cooked pumpkin along with hamburger stew. Rutabagas with Crisp Shallots (page 130).

Dinner in a Pumpkin

Serves 6 to 8

1 medium pumpkin, about 5 pounds

1 onion, chopped to make about 1 cup

2 tablespoons vegetable oil

1½ pounds lean ground beef

2 tablespoons soy sauce

2 tablespoons brown sugar

1 (4-ounce) can sliced mushrooms,

    drained

1 (10¾-ounce) can cream

    of chicken soup

2 cups cooked rice

1 (8-ounce) can sliced water

    chestnuts, drained

The photograph to accompany this recipe was nearly a traffic stopper. The pumpkin, filled with a rice and hamburger stew, was transported in the trunk of the car, along with appropriate props. We drove all around downtown looking for the perfect location until a length of old brick sidewalk was spotted. There were even a few yellow chrysanthemums to complete the fall scene. But passersby weren't sure if we were setting up a lunch stand or having a picnic. Even without a pumpkin, this is a great family casserole to bake in a standard baking dish.

Cut off top of pumpkin. Thoroughly clean out seeds and pulp.

Sauté onion in oil in large skillet. Add ground beef and brown. Drain off all drippings. Add soy sauce, brown sugar, sliced mushrooms, and cream of chicken soup. Simmer 10 minutes. Stir in cooked rice and water chestnuts. Mix well.

Spoon mixture into pumpkin shell. Replace top. Bake on cookie sheet in 350-degree oven about 1 hour, or until the pumpkin flesh is tender.

Serve directly from the shell, scooping out some cooked pumpkin along with the hamburger stew.

photo page 52

Barbecued Short Ribs

Serves 4 to 5

3 pounds short ribs of beef

2 tablespoons shortening

1 medium onion, chopped

¼ cup vinegar

2 tablespoons brown sugar

1 cup ketchup

½ cup water

¼ teaspoon hot pepper sauce

1 teaspoon prepared mustard

½ cup diced celery

1 teaspoon salt

Consider short ribs for a weekend meal because they take a long time to cook. Just leave them in the oven and go about your business, knowing that it will take two or three hours before the fork slips into them easily, indicating that they are tender perfect. The ribs are cut from the chuck, which gives them a similar rich, beef flavor.

Have ribs cut into sections 2 to 3 inches long. Melt shortening in heavy frying pan. Brown ribs. Add onion and cook 2 to 3 minutes; do not brown. Add remaining ingredients.

Cover and cook slowly on top of range or bake in large casserole in a moderate oven of 325 degrees for 3 hours, or longer, until tender.

Barbecued Brisket

1 (6-to-7 pound) brisket of beef

1/4 cup cider vinegar

1 1/2 cups water

1/4 cup sugar

4 teaspoons prepared mustard

1 teaspoon salt

1/4 teaspoon pepper

2 large lemon slices, chopped

2 medium onions, sliced

1/2 cup margarine

1 cup ketchup

3 tablespoons Worcestershire sauce

Long, slow roasting is the secret to a tender brisket that is cooked the day before it is served in a barbecue sauce.

Cover brisket with water in pan, and roast, with lid on in 300-degree oven for 3 1/2 to 5 hours or until tender. Cool overnight. Remove from liquid.

Slice thin, against the grain. Simmer all ingredients but ketchup and Worcestershire sauce 20 minutes. Then add them and mix well. Place sliced meat in sauce and simmer a few minutes to heat through.

Best Meat Loaf

2 pounds ground chuck

1/2 pound ground veal

1/2 pound ground pork

2 eggs, beaten

1 chopped onion

1 cup plain bread crumbs

1/2 of (12-ounce) jar of
   mild thick-and-chunky salsa

1 teaspoon salt

1/2 teaspoon pepper

1/4 cup parsley flakes

American cooks began to re-judge meat loaf in the 1980s, and midwest cooks were first in line to show how it is made. Of the 600 recipes received in a Blade contest, this recipe, prepared by Nancy Meyer, Findlay, Ohio, was judged best.

In a large mixing bowl, combine ground meats and mix well. Add eggs, chopped onion, and bread crumbs. Mix well by hand. Stir in salsa, salt, pepper, and parsley flakes. Knead by hand for at least five minutes the way bread dough is kneaded.

Shape into a loaf and bake on a rack in shallow roasting pan. Bake 1 hour in 350-degree oven. Cool 5 minutes before slicing.

Erie Street Chili Mac

Serves 6

2 pounds economy hamburger

Salt

1 tablespoon cumin seeds

1 tablespoon ground red pepper

1 tablespoon paprika

½ teaspoon white pepper

3 diced garlic cloves

4 tablespoons chili powder

2 tablespoons sugar

3 (1 pound) cans pinto or red beans

Cooked spaghetti or macaroni

Anyone who is even thinking about counting fat grams won't like it. Economy ground beef is required here to insure that there is plenty of grease in the meat, and some recipes even call for suet in addition to the ground beef. It is named for a downtown Toledo café that remains a legend because of Chili Mac, although few people can remember exactly where it was located.

Brown hamburger on low heat in large skillet; add all ingredients except beans and spaghetti and simmer for 3 hours. Add water to make sauce as needed and do not remove grease.

For chili, heat 3 cans pinto or red beans to boiling; spoon beans into chili bowl with slotted spoon and spoon meat mixture on top.

To make Chili Mac, mix meat mixture and beans. Make a nest of spaghetti on plate and spoon chili mixture over it.

London Broil

1 (1¾ to 2 pounds) flank steak

1 teaspoon salt

½ teaspoon pepper

¼ teaspoon each: basil and rosemary

1 garlic clove, crushed

½ onion, chopped

2 tablespoons red wine vinegar

4 tablespoons salad oil

The broiled flank steak is an old classic that meets today's dietary requirements for small portions of lean meat. The flank is a lean cut that is cut very thin. This one is nicely seasoned. Arrange an assortment of vegetables around the sliced meat on a platter. Redskins, parsnips, carrots, and Brussels sprouts, and baby eggplant in season give a variety of taste and color to the presentation.

Combine marinade ingredients in flat dish. Marinate steak in it, turning occasionally, for at least 2 hours. Remove from marinade and broil about 3 inches from heat. Broil 5 minutes, turn and brush with marinade, and broil another 3 to 5 minutes.

Cut into very thin slices across the grain.

Marinated Beef Tenderloin

Serves 8 to 10

1 head garlic, approximately 14 cloves,
  mashed

2 cups mild sorghum molasses

1 cup soy sauce

1/2 cup sherry, brandy, or dark rum

1 cup brown sugar

1/2 teaspoon sweet basil

1/4 teaspoon fennel

1/2 teaspoon thyme

1 teaspoon black pepper

1 (3-pound) whole beef tenderloin,
  membrane removed

When they are asked for their favorite recipe, Geneva and Bruce Williams, who operate Gourmet Curiosities Creative Cooking School, say, "We have many, but the tenderloin definitely is one of our favorites." Molasses is the surprise ingredient in this marinade. The Williamses recommend that the tenderloin be served with French bread and an herb butter.

To make marinade, combine garlic, molasses, soy sauce, sherry, and brown sugar. Pulverize basil, fennel, thyme, and black pepper and add to marinade.

Marinate the tenderloin with mixture. For smaller pieces of meat, use only enough marinade to cover; unused marinade can be stored in the refrigerator indefinitely.

Broil the tenderloin about 5 minutes on each side for rare, 11 minutes on each side for medium. Cut the meat across the grain into slices and serve with French bread and herb butter.

HERB BUTTER: Cream 3/4 cup butter with 1 tablespoon minced watercress leaves, 1 tablespoon minced chives or green onion tops, 1 tablespoon minced parsley, and 1 tablespoon lemon juice; add salt and pepper to taste.

Mexican-Style Lasagna

Serves 6

1 tablespoon vegetable oil

1 large onion, chopped

1 green pepper, chopped

1 garlic clove, minced

1 teaspoon dried leaf oregano, crumbled

1 pound ground beef

1 (1-pound) can tomatoes, drained and chopped

1 (8-ounce) can tomato sauce

1 cup sour cream

3/4 teaspoon hot pepper sauce, or more

10 (5-inch) tortillas

1 (1-pound) can pinto beans, drained

2 cups shredded Cheddar cheese

It came as no surprise to Toledoans that Mexican food would make a hit nationally. The craze hit here in the early 60s when family restaurants were opened by farm workers, and it hasn't stopped. We still are wild about all the things that can happen to, on, and with tortillas. Here is just one example of how they can be used in a make-ahead, family dish.

Sauté onion, green pepper, and garlic in oil in large skillet. Stir in oregano. Add beef; break up with fork, and cook through.

In a medium bowl, combine tomatoes, tomato sauce, sour cream, and hot pepper sauce.

Cut each tortilla in half. Arrange 10 halves on shallow oblong baking dish with the rounded sides coming above the edges of the pan. Spread half the meat mixture over tortillas. Top with half of the pinto beans, half the tomato sauce mixture, and 1 cup shredded cheese. Repeat with remaining ingredients.

Bake 30 minutes in 350-degree oven. Let stand 10 minutes before cutting into squares.

No-Peek Beef Stew

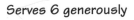

Serves 6 generously

2 pounds beef stew meat

4 or 5 celery ribs, cut into
    1-inch pieces

4 or 5 potatoes, pared and cut up

3 large onions, peeled and cut up

1 can beef broth

1 (1-pound) can stewed tomatoes

4 or more carrots, pared and cut up

1 teaspoon salt

Pepper to taste

5 tablespoons tapioca

A dependable recipe that lets the cook do other chores, even run an errand or two, while the beef and vegetables cook and thicken with tapioca.

Combine all ingredients in a roaster with a tight-fitting cover or a Dutch oven. Bake 4 hours in 325-degree oven. Do not open oven door while it is cooking.

Pinwheel Meat Loaf

½ cup milk

2 cups cubed Italian or French bread,
    crusts removed

1½ pounds lean ground beef

½ pound Italian sausage,
    casing removed, crumbled

2 eggs, slightly beaten

2 tablespoons chopped parsley

1 teaspoon minced garlic

Salt and pepper

2 cups water

1 tablespoon butter

1 package rice and sauce, Cajun-style

2 (10-ounce) packages frozen, chopped
    spinach, thawed and squeezed dry

Three layers—meat, Cajun seasoned rice, and spinach—take this from standard meat loaf status to company fare. It takes a little doing, but it can be assembled, wrapped well, and refrigerated until roasting time the next day. The beauty is in the slices that display the three layers.

Pour milk over bread cubes; mash with fork. Add all but rice mix and spinach. Mix well.

Moisten 12-inch square piece of aluminum foil. Place meat mixture on it. Cover with 12-by-14-inch waxed paper, moistened with water. Press meat into 12-by-13-inch rectangle. Refrigerate at least 2 hours to chill well. Boil and stir rice and sauce, butter, and water 10 minutes. Chill.

Remove waxed paper from meat. Spread spinach over beef, leaving 1-inch border. Spread rice evenly over spinach. Roll up on long side, using foil as a guide, but pull off foil as it rolls. Seal ends and seam tightly. Place seam side down on 9-by-13-inch baking pan. Bake 1-hour in 350-degree oven.

Pot Roast with Prunes and Wine

Serves 8

4 pounds beef chuck

2 tablespoons shortening

1 large onion, chopped

1 (20-ounce) can tomatoes

1/4 cup water

1 cup red wine

1 1/2 cup dry prunes

1 teaspoon salt

Pepper to taste

1 (8-ounce) package noodles

1/4 cup grated Parmesan cheese

Prunes and red wine with a chuck roast? That's the same question asked in 1960 when Mrs. John Sharon, Toledo, submitted it to The Blade recipe contest, which drew about 4,000 recipes. Curiosity prevailed. It was tested, tasted, and won the Grand Prize, hands down.

Brown meat in shortening. Add chopped onion, tomatoes, and water; cook, covered, for 2 hours. Add wine, prunes, salt, and pepper. Continue to cook until prunes are tender.

Cook noodles in boiling, salted water; drain, place on platter. Sprinkle with grated cheese, top with sliced meat, and drizzle with all the sauce from the meat pan.

This recipe may be prepared on the top burner if a heavy cooking skillet is used, or it can be prepared in the oven at 325 degrees.

Sauerbraten and Spaetzle

Serves 8

3 pounds beef rump roast

Salt and pepper

3 bay leaves

1/2 teaspoon peppercorns

8 whole cloves

2 medium onions, sliced

1 small carrot, minced

1 celery rib

1 1/2 cups red wine vinegar

2 1/2 cups water

1/4 cup butter

Gingersnap gravy accompanies this Sauerbraten, or "sour roast" in German. The meat marinates for two days in a sweet-sour marinade. Spaetzles are tiny dumplings or noodles, the perfect accompaniment for this classic dish.

Rub meat with 1 teaspoon salt and 1/2 teaspoon pepper; place in ceramic or glass bowl. Add spices and vegetables. Heat vinegar and water to boiling; pour hot over meat. Let cool. Cover and refrigerate 48 hours, but turn meat twice each day. Remove meat from marinade and dry with paper towels. Brown meat in butter in Dutch oven. Strain marinade and pour over meat. Cover and simmer slowly 2 to 3 hours, or until fork tender. Remove to warm platter. Slice and keep warm.

GINGERSNAP GRAVY: Melt 2 tablespoons sugar in skillet and stir until it browns. Gradually stir in 1 1/2 cups hot marinade and 1/2 cup hot water. Add 2/3 cup gingersnap crumbs (about 8 cookies) and cook and stir until mixture thickens. Add 1/2 cup sour cream. Season with salt and ladle over sauerbraten slices and spaetzle.

SPAETZLE: Mix 3 cups flour and 1 tablespoon salt. Add 3 beaten eggs, 1/2 cup water, and 1 tablespoon oil. Beat well. Drop batter by teaspoon into boiling, salted water. Cook 10 minutes; drain. Rinse with cold water and drain well. Gently stir in 1 teaspoon oil to keep them from sticking together.

Tailgate Sausage Cookout

Serves 8 to 12

2 medium onions, sliced thin

4 fully cooked bratwurst

4 fully cooked Polish sausages

4 fully cooked knackwurst

2 cans beer

2 garlic cloves, halved

1 teaspoon crushed red pepper

When the leaves begin to turn in autumn, and there's a nip in the air, midwesterners begin to think about sausages, especially the kinds brought to us by the large German and Polish populations in the region. You don't have to take a grill to a tailgate picnic at a football game to try this recipe. It works just as well stove-top or in the oven.

Place half the onions on bottom of large flat pan with tight fitting lid. Arrange sausages on top. Combine beer, garlic, and red pepper and pour over sausages. Top with remaining onion slices.

Cover tightly and refrigerate 6 hours or overnight. Transport container in cooler. Cook sausages over charcoal 4 inches from the heat for at least 15 minutes. Serve in buns.

Tony Packo's Stuffed Cabbage

Serves 6

1 (3 pound) head cabbage, core removed

1 pound ground pork

1 pound ground beef

2 eggs, slightly beaten

2 medium onions, chopped, divided

1 garlic clove, minced

3 teaspoons salt

1 teaspoon pepper

2 tablespoons paprika

1 cup rice, soaked in cold water 15 minutes

1 pound sauerkraut

1 (1-pound) can whole tomatoes,
    mashed, juice retained

1 (10-ounce) can tomato soup

2 tablespoons sugar

Sour cream sauce (below)

A 62-year-old Toledo tradition, Tony Packo's is second only to the Museum of Art as the city's main attraction. The Hungarian café is famous for hot dogs with a meat sauce and pickles, which are now on the retail market. But when it comes to recipes, stuffed cabbage is the only one the Packo family releases.

To remove leaves, immerse cabbage in boiling water for 10 minutes. Drain. Remove large leaves and cut out large vein from each in a triangular cut. As the leaves get smaller, overlap two leaves for one roll.

Combine meat, eggs, 1 chopped onion, garlic, 2 teaspoons salt, pepper, and paprika. Rinse rice in cold water; drain. Add to meat mixture and thoroughly mix.

Flatten leaves and place about ½ cup meat mixture on each. Roll up and tuck in sides as it is rolled. Continue until meat and cabbage leaves are used.

After the good leaves are used, chop remaining cabbage and combine with sauerkraut, tomatoes and juice, tomato soup, sugar, and remaining onion and salt. Add water to cover the top of the rolls. Layer cabbage rolls in large cooking pot. Pour kraut-tomato mixture over rolls.

Cover and cook on low heat at least 2 hours. Add water as needed so that the rolls always are covered as they cook. Serve with sour cream sauce.

SOUR CREAM SAUCE: Sauté 2 small chopped onions in ¼ cup butter. Stir in 1 tablespoon sour cream and 1 (1-pound) can whole tomatoes, mashed, and their juice. Serve warm.

Woody's Barbecue Sauce

2 quarts water

4 (12-ounce) cans tomato paste

4 lemons, cut into eighths

3 garlic cloves, minced

2 medium onions, chopped fine

12 large bay leaves, broken

2 teaspoons celery salt

4 teaspoons salt

3 teaspoons cayenne pepper

3¼ cups white vinegar

3 cups light brown sugar, packed

The first time this recipe was written was when it was published in 1981. Before sharing his secret recipe, Herbert D. Woodhull emphasized his rib cooking rules:

"No boiling of the ribs first, that takes away the flavor. Don't put the sauce on until the ribs are almost done, probably the last 15 minutes. And when the sauce is on you've got to watch them. You can't go rambling around and go do the laundry or the ribs will burn before you know it."

Put all of the ingredients into a large pan. Stir to combine. Bring to a boil, but reduce to a simmer and cook, simmering, 45 minutes.

This keeps well indefinitely in a tightly covered container in the refrigerator. Use on spareribs, chicken, or frankfurters.

Swiss Cheese Fondue

Serves 2

1 (8-ounce) package Swiss cheese
   slices, cut into strips

1 tablespoon flour

1 garlic clove, cut in half

1 cup dry white wine

2 tablespoons kirsch, if desired

Dash nutmeg, if desired

Salt and pepper

French Bread

Vegetables to dip

Dust off the fondue pot for a return engagement of a 70s entertaining custom. Who says cheese fondue is too simple for special guests? This one is made with white wine and kirsch. Kirsch, short for Kirschwasser, is a dry, colorless brandy made from the fermented juice of the black morella cherry. It is primarily a product of Switzerland and the Black Forest region of Germany.

Toss cheese with flour. Rub inside of fondue pot or electric skillet with garlic. Add wine and heat until bubbles rise to the surface.

Add ½ cup of the cheese mixture. Stir constantly until melted. Repeat until all the cheese has been added. Stir in kirsch and seasonings. Keep fondue hot while serving. Skewer chunks of bread and cherry tomatoes, broccoli, and cauliflower florets, and other vegetables to dip into the fondue pot.

Use as an appetizer or main course.

American Brunswick Stew

Serves 10 to 12

2¼ pounds chicken thighs

2½ pounds chicken breasts

½ pound bacon, chopped

6 quarts water

1 rabbit, cut into parts

1 pound frozen green lima beans

1 (17-ounce) can whole kernel corn

1 (28-ounce) can diced tomatoes, drained,
   or use fresh tomatoes

2 teaspoons salt

½ teaspoon ground red pepper

1 teaspoon pepper

4 cups mashed potatoes

2 tablespoons butter

4 slices white bread, torn into large pieces

Students of American culinary history appreciate the ingenuity of colonial cooks who tapped limited resources. If the family hunter brought home a bag of squirrels today, would 20th century cooks invent a dish as nicely balanced as the Brunswick stew? It originated in Brunswick County, Virginia, in 1828 as a way to use squirrel meat. Squirrel is omitted in revised recipes in favor of more available, and palatable, substitutions. Chicken and rabbit work well. It is also interesting that colonial cooks used corn and limas, the two native vegetables, in the concoction, and that mashed potatoes and bread are thickening agents. This recipe uses frozen corn and limas.

Put chicken, bacon, and water into large soup pot. Cover and bring to boil. Cook until chicken is very tender. Cook rabbit parts in another pan, covered with water. When done, drain off juices. Remove meat from chicken and rabbit pieces and return meat to the broth in which chicken was cooked.

Add lima beans, corn, tomatoes, and seasonings. Cook another 25 minutes. Stir in potatoes, butter, and bread pieces and simmer until they are absorbed in the stew. Serve very hot in soup plates with cornbread. NOTE: Chicken alone can be used in place of rabbit and chicken.

Chicken Chasseur

Serves 6

6 skinless, boneless chicken

    breast halves

1 tablespoon vegetable oil

½ cup sliced green onions

½ teaspoon Italian seasoning

2 (10 ¾-ounce) cans condensed

    cream of mushroom soup, undiluted

⅓ cup dry white wine

½ cup cut-up canned tomatoes

1½ cups water

2 tablespoons butter

½ teaspoon salt

1 cup couscous

2 tablespoons chopped parsley

Canned cream of mushroom soup and couscous in the same recipe cross cultures and contribute to an easily prepared main dish. The soup is the base for a sauce in which chicken simmers, and all is served over couscous.

Brown chicken in skillet in oil. Remove and set aside. In same skillet, sauté onions and seasoning. Stir in soup, wine and tomatoes. Return chicken to skillet. Simmer, covered, 30 to 35 minutes until chicken is tender.

Bring water, butter, and salt to a boil. Stir in couscous; cover. Remove from heat and let stand 5 minutes. Just before serving, stir parsley into sauce and fluff couscous with a fork. Serve chicken and sauce over couscous.

Chicken Enchiladas

Serves 15

1 teaspoon oil

2 (4-ounce) cans green chilies

1 large garlic clove, minced

1 (28-ounce) can whole tomatoes

2 cups chopped onion

2 teaspoons salt

½ teaspoon oregano

3 cups shredded, cooked chicken

2 cups sour cream

2 cups grated Cheddar cheese

¼ cup oil

15 corn tortillas

"I can tell you one thing," Liza Ashley said from the governor's mansion in Little Rock, Arkansas, "Governor Clinton likes broccoli." Mrs. Ashley was the cook for the Clintons for 10 years before they moved into the White House, and she wanted the press to know that the new president did not have tastes similar to the outgoing head of state. Chicken Enchiladas, she said, were President Clinton's favorite entrée, but to make the meal complete, lemon chess pie would be the perfect ending.

Heat oil in a large skillet. Drain chilies, remove seeds, and chop. Sauté chilies and garlic in oil until garlic is softened.

Drain and break up tomatoes, reserving ½ cup juice. To chilies and garlic add tomatoes, onion, 1 teaspoon salt, oregano, and reserved tomato juice. Simmer, uncovered, until thick, about 30 minutes. Set aside.

In a bowl, stir together chicken, sour cream, grated Cheddar cheese, and 1 teaspoon salt. Heat ¼ cup oil in a saucepan or skillet. Dip tortillas in oil just until they become limp; drain well on paper towels.

Spoon some of the chicken mixture onto each tortilla. Roll up and arrange seam side down in a 9-by-13-inch baking dish.

Pour tomato-chili sauce over enchiladas and bake at 350 degrees until heated through, about 20 minutes.

Chicken Parmesan Rolls

Serves 4

4 whole chicken breasts, boned,

    skinned, and halved

1 stick melted butter, or more

1 cup bread crumbs

1 cup grated Parmesan cheese

Slivered almonds

Additional melted butter

If there's no need for another recipe for boneless, skinless chicken breasts, turn the page. Otherwise, refer to this recipe for an easy but elegant way to present a favorite cut of chicken, rolled and baked in Parmesan and butter with an almond topping.

Dip each chicken breast half in melted butter. Combine equal amounts of bread crumbs and Parmesan cheese and mix well. Coat buttered chicken pieces on both sides in crumb mixture and roll up tightly. Line up in baking dish so that they touch. (It is usually not necessary to secure the rolled breasts with picks if the seam side is placed down.) Sprinkle with almonds and with more melted butter. If necessary, cover and refrigerate.

Bake 1 hour in 350-degree oven. If desired, season chicken breasts first with salt and pepper, but because of the salt in the butter and bread crumbs, it is not necessary.

Lemon Chicken Cutlets

6 halves chicken breast, boneless

    and skinless

1/4 cup flour

1/2 teaspoon salt

1/8 teaspoon pepper

3 tablespoons butter

1 cup water

1 chicken-flavored bouillon cube

Juice of 1/2 lemon

2 small lemons, sliced thin

Thank the Toledo Hospital Auxiliary for this easy elegant recipe. After it's prepared the first time you'll want to invite someone over so you can make and enjoy it again.

Pound chicken breast halves thin. Mix flour, salt, and pepper. Coat chicken. Reserve remaining flour. Heat butter; add chicken and brown lightly. Remove chicken.

Reduce heat, stir remaining flour into drippings. Add water, bouillon cube, and juice of half a lemon. Return chicken to skillet. Add lemon slices. Cover and simmer 5 minutes or until chicken is fork-tender.

Scalloped Chicken and Stuffing

Serves 12

1 (8-ounce) package herb-seasoned stuffing

3 cups cubed cooked chicken or turkey

½ cup butter

½ cup flour

¼ teaspoon salt

Dash pepper

4 cups chicken broth

6 slightly beaten eggs

Pimiento-mushroom sauce

We cannot totally discount packaged foods and expect always to be scratch cooks like our grandmothers were. It is quite probable that they also would have depended on convenience foods had they been available in their day. The food editor's Michigan farm grandmother - who cooked the chickens she raised for threshers and family, made dressing with homemade bread and sauces for it with cream from the barn - would have no doubt been delighted for the opportunity to follow this recipe with short cuts.

Spread stuffing in greased, 13-by-9-inch baking pan. Top with a layer of chicken. In large saucepan, melt butter and blend in flour and seasonings. Add broth; cook and stir until mixture thickens. Stir small amount of hot mixture into eggs; add to remaining hot mixture. Pour over chicken.

Bake 1 hour in 325-degree oven, or until knife inserted in center comes out clean. Let stand 5 minutes before cutting into squares. Serve with pimiento-mushroom sauce, if desired.

PIMIENTO-MUSHROOM SAUCE: Combine 1 can cream of mushroom soup, ¼ cup milk, 1 cup commercial sour cream, and ¼ cup chopped pimiento. Heat thoroughly.

Slow Cooker Chicken

1 (4-pound) chicken, in serving pieces

    (if desired, with skin removed)

2 cups chicken broth

1 onion, studded with 1 whole clove

2 carrots, cut in half

2 celery stalks, cut in half

4 parsley sprigs, 1 bay leaf, and

    1/4 teaspoon thyme tied in a bag

Salt and white pepper

1 package thawed frozen peas

Slow cookers were the hot gift item for Christmas, 1976, and recipes such as this were published to warm up the recipients to their new appliances. Set the alarm early to gather the ingredients for a chicken stew that will be ready eight hours later, just when the after school and after work crowds are starving.

Combine all but peas in slow cooker. Cover and cook on low 8 to 10 hours. Add peas during last hour. Remove herb bag before serving.

Stuffed Chicken Breasts

2 cups chopped celery

1 cup chopped onion

½ cup butter

1 envelope dry chicken noodle soup

3 cups water or chicken stock

4 cups dry bread cubes

2 slightly beaten eggs

Salt and pepper

8 to 10 whole boneless chicken breasts

Butter to baste

Serving as food manager of the Laurel Hills Tennis Club wasn't enough to satisfy Lela Tuller's appetite for cooking, and so she taught classes. These boneless chicken breasts wrapped around a moist dressing were popular with students and club guests. Note it doesn't call for skinless chicken; this recipe comes from the 60s.

Sauté celery and onion in butter. Cook noodle soup, using 3 cups water or stock. Add sautéed vegetables and soup to bread cubes; mix well. Add beaten eggs. Season and mix. It will be very moist.

Spread out chicken breasts, flatten and season. Place portion of stuffing on each. Roll up and pin securely. Place, pin side down, in open pan. Bake 25 minutes in 350-degree oven. During baking, baste with butter.

Spicy Thai-Style Chicken and Rice

Yields 5 servings

5 chicken breast halves,

    skinned and boned

1/4 cup reduced sodium soy sauce

2 teaspoons peanut or vegetable oil

1 cup rice

1 large garlic clove, minced

2¼ cups chicken broth

2 tablespoons creamy peanut butter

1/2 teaspoon red pepper flakes, or

    1/4 teaspoon ground red pepper

1½ cups pea pods, cut in halves

1 tablespoon finely shredded fresh ginger

1 small red pepper, cut into short,

    thin strips

2 tablespoons peanut halves, if desired

Thai foods are identified by their hot, spicy, well-balanced seasonings. They also teach Americans that there's life for peanut butter beyond sandwiches. The Thai use the peanut spread in sauces and often season it with red peppers, as it is here in a chicken and rice skillet entrée.

Combine chicken and soy sauce in shallow bowl. Set aside. Heat oil in 10-inch skillet over medium heat. Add rice and garlic. Cook and stir 1 minute.

Stir in broth, peanut butter, and pepper flakes. Bring to a boil and stir until peanut butter is melted. Place chicken over rice mixture. Add soy sauce from chicken to skillet. Reduce heat. Cover and simmer 20 minutes, or until chicken is thoroughly done.

Stir in pea pods and ginger. Sprinkle with pepper strips. Remove from heat. Let stand, covered, until all liquid is absorbed. Sprinkle with peanuts, if desired.

Yorkshire Chicken

Serves 6

1/3 cup flour

1 teaspoon salt

1/4 teaspoon pepper

1 1/2 teaspoons crumbled leaf sage

1 (3 1/2 -pound) fryer, cut up, skin

removed, or parts such as boneless,

skinless, chicken breasts

1/4 cup vegetable oil

Yorkshire pudding (recipe below)

In 1976, Family Circle magazine asked The Blade food editor for a low-cost recipe. Yorkshire Chicken was submitted not just because it is an economy main dish, but because it is elegant and just might be the food editor's favorite. English Yorkshire pudding, usually reserved as a roast beef accompaniment, bakes high and crisp on top of sage seasoned chicken parts.

Combine flour, salt, pepper, and sage in bag or on waxed paper. Coat chicken parts with flour. Pour oil into 9-by-13-inch baking pan or a 2 1/2 to 3-quart casserole. Place chicken parts in oil and turn to coat both sides. Bake chicken in 400-degree oven 40 minutes.

The dish can be prepared in advance to this point, covered, and refrigerated. If this is done, reheat it in 400-degree oven before pouring pudding over it.

Pour Yorkshire pudding batter over chicken. It is essential that the fat and the juices from pre-baking be left in pan to insure a good pudding. Return chicken and pudding to the oven and bake an additional 25 minutes until it is puffed up and nicely browned.

YORKSHIRE PUDDING: Sift 1 cup flour, 1 teaspoon baking powder, and 1 teaspoon salt into medium bowl. Gradually beat in 1 1/2 cups milk, 3 eggs, and 1/4 cup chopped fresh parsley or 4 teaspoons dried parsley flakes.

Green Peppercorn Duck Madagascar

Serves 4

1 duck, about 5 pounds

½ orange, cut into 2 pieces

1 celery stalk, with leaves

Salt and pepper

½ onion, cut in half

1 sprig parsley

Stock:

1 additional onion, cut in half

1 additional celery stalk, with leaves

2 carrots, chopped

2 sprigs parsley

1 bay leaf

5 black peppercorns

1 teaspoon salt

2 cups dry red wine

1 cup water

Duck giblets

3 tablespoons green peppercorns

1 tablespoon flour

1 tablespoon butter, preferably unsalted

The day after former White House Chef Annemarie Huste demonstrated this show-stopper recipe at the 1973 Blade Food Fair, local stores ran out of green peppercorns, and Toledoans have been making it ever since.

Combine stock ingredients except the green peppercorns, flour, and butter in heavy saucepan. Bring to boil, simmer for 1 hour. Strain stock. Add green peppercorns. Combine flour and butter, add to thicken sauce.

Rub duck inside and out with salt and pepper. Stuff with orange, celery, onion, parsley. Close opening with metal skewer.

Place duck on back on rack, in roasting pan. Roast for 15 minutes in 450-degree oven. Reduce oven temperature to 350-degrees. Remove drippings; baste duck with stock every 15 minutes and bake for another hour.

Asparagus-Ham-Chicken Quiche

Serves 6 to 8

1 unbaked, deep, (10-inch) pastry shell

3/4 cup diced, cooked chicken

    or turkey

1/4 cup diced ham

2 cups asparagus, cut in

    1/2-inch pieces

1/2 cup grated Swiss cheese

3 eggs

2 cups milk or half and half

Pinch each: nutmeg and white pepper

3 to 4 asparagus spears for garnish

When entertaining at a Sunday brunch is on the agenda, circle this quiche as a candidate for the main dish. It cuts beautifully into slices that show off ham, chicken, and asparagus.

It is best to cook asparagus al dente and drain it well. Otherwise, during cooking and baking, moisture from it may upset the custard. Brush pastry with an egg white to reduce sogginess.

Arrange chicken, ham, asparagus, and cheese in pie shell. Beat eggs and add milk and seasonings. Pour over filling. Pour into pie shell. If desired, decorate top with asparagus spears.

Bake 15 minutes in 425-degree oven; reduce heat to 300 degrees and bake 30 to 40 minutes more, until a knife inserted in center comes out clean.

End of the Garden Frittata

Serves 6

2 teaspoons butter

1½ cups sliced zucchini, not pared

1 cup fresh corn kernels

½ cup chopped sweet red pepper

¼ cup chopped onion

¼ teaspoon oregano leaves, crushed

4 eggs

¼ cup milk

¼ cup shredded Cheddar cheese

Frittatas are an excellent way to trap fresh vegetables in a quick supper dish. Mix and match the vegetables according to what's in the garden or the crisper. Frittatas are the Italian version of omelets, but they are easier because they don't have to be folded over a filling. Frittatas are served flat and crisp.

Melt butter in 10-inch skillet. Add vegetables and oregano. Cover and cook over medium heat, stirring occasionally, until tender but still crisp.

Whisk eggs with milk and pour over vegetables. Cook over low heat until eggs are almost set. Sprinkle cheese over top. Broil about 6 inches from heat just until cheese is melted.

Cut into wedges and serve from the skillet.

Overnight Sausage-and-Eggs Soufflé

Serves 6 to 8

6 eggs, beaten

2 cups milk

1 teaspoon salt

1 tablespoon dry mustard

6 slices white bread, cubed

1 pound mild sausage, browned,

    drained, cooled, and crumbled

1 cup grated Cheddar cheese

Here is a sausage and egg soufflé that bakes high and light. Many a host has been rescued from morning breakfast hassle by a casserole that sleeps while the guests do and is oven ready in the morning. This well may be the recipe that has been shared by more people than any other in this cookbook.

Combine eggs, milk, salt, mustard, and bread cubes; add sausage and stir in cheese. Pour into lightly oiled soufflé dish. Cover and refrigerate overnight.

Bake 45 minutes in 350-degree oven.

Zucchini Impossible Pie

Serves 6

3 cups zucchini, sliced very thin

1/2 cup baking mix

1/2 cup grated Parmesan cheese

1/2 cup oil

1/2 cup chopped onion

6 eggs, slightly beaten

1/2 teaspoon salt

1/2 teaspoon oregano

In this, and other impossible pie formulas, baking mix magically falls to the bottom of the baking pan to form a crust. Impossible pies are examples of grassroots recipes that creep through the country over backyard fences and from state to state. They pick up speed as their success is reported, but they vanish as other newsy recipes appear.

Mix all ingredients but zucchini, then add it and pour into greased 9-by-13-inch pan. Bake about 30 minutes in 350-degree oven. Serve warm or cold.

Crab Elegant

Serves 6

---

1 cup sliced celery

1/4 cup butter

1 cup sliced fresh mushrooms, or

    1 (4-ounce) can mushrooms, drained

1/4 cup sliced green onions

3 tablespoons flour

3/4 teaspoons salt

Dash white pepper

1 cup milk

1/2 cup half and half

1/4 cup sherry (optional)

1/2 teaspoon Worcestershire sauce

2 cups crabmeat

2 tablespoons diced pimientos

6 servings hot, fluffy rice

1 ripe avocado, peeled and sliced

Two cups of crabmeat stretch to serve six people in a main dish rich with cream and delicately flavored with sherry. Pimiento adds color, and avocado slices are recommended as a pretty garnish.

Cook celery in butter until tender. Add mushrooms and onion; cook until tender. Blend in flour, salt, and pepper. Stir in milk and half and half. Cook until thickened, stirring constantly. Add sherry, Worcestershire sauce, crabmeat, and pimiento. Mix carefully.

Place over low heat; bring to serving temperature, stirring often. Serve over rice. Garnish with avocado.

Baked Ohio Trout

Serves 2

1 (1-pound) whole trout, cleaned

1 bunch fresh basil

1 lemon, sliced thin

¼ cup Ohio dry white wine

Ohio Governor George Voinovich's favorite promotion of Ohio foods extends beyond speeches, visiting farms, and pushing the Buy Ohio program. He occasionally puts on an apron and demonstrates an all-Ohio recipe. The trout recipe is from the governor's file of favorites. You can be sure rice is not on the governor's menu. It is not grown in the state.

Wash trout in running water; wipe dry inside and out. Place trout on piece of foil large enough to make packet. Clean basil and pick off leaves from stems. Slice lemon very thin. Lace cavity of trout with lemon slices and basil leaves. Pour wine over fish and wrap up foil around trout to form a loose packet. Place in baking dish and bake 20 minutes in 350-degree oven.

Remove from foil and place on serving platter. Place 3 lemon slices on cooked trout and 2 bunches fresh parsley. Serve with pasta, some of which is Ohio-made.

Crab-Stuffed Walleye

Serves 8

1 small onion, finely chopped

½ cup chopped mushrooms

½ stick butter

1 cup soft bread crumbs

1 cup crabmeat

2 eggs, beaten

1 tablespoon chopped parsley

Dash ground red pepper

3 tablespoons sherry

3 to 4 pounds ready to cook

    whole pickerel or any firm-fleshed fish

Butter, melted

Lake Erie is a gold mine for walleye, and northwest Ohioans are hooked on the beautiful white fish. Broiling fillets or deep frying battered whole walleye to a golden crispness are the common cooking methods. But for special occasions, the local fish goes gourmet with a crabmeat stuffing and sauce.

Sauté onion and mushrooms in butter for 5 minutes. Add rest of stuffing ingredients; mix. Stuff into cleaned fish, close opening with skewers.

Bake in buttered baking dish for 1 hour in 350-degree oven, brushing fish with butter during baking. Serve with mushroom-crab sauce, if desired.

MUSHROOM-CRAB SAUCE: Sauté 1 small chopped onion and ½ cup chopped mushrooms in ½ cup butter. Add 2 tablespoons flour; stir. Add 2 tablespoons light cream; cook, stirring until thickened. Add ¼ cup crabmeat and dashes of nutmeg and thyme. Stir in a little basil, fresh if possible, and 1 tablespoon sherry.

Crabmeat, Northwood-Style

Serves 6

6 tablespoons butter

½ cup flour

1¼ cups hot milk

1 cup warm cream

¼ cup bread crumbs

2 tablespoons grated

    Parmesan cheese

1 ½ tablespoons sherry

1 tablespoon finely chopped

    green pepper

1 tablespoon finely chopped

    green onion

1 teaspoon Worcestershire sauce

½ teaspoon curry powder

1 teaspoon Dijon mustard

2 cups crabmeat

Grated Parmesan cheese

When Northwood-style is attached to the name of any dish in the Toledo area, it puts the Gen Dokurno stamp of excellence on it. Mrs. Dokurno has a 60-year record as an outstanding Ohio restaurateur at the Northwood Inn and the Northwood Villa. This appetizer or main dish casserole is typical of Northwood crab specialties. This is not the recipe to substitute low-fat milk. Stick with Mrs. Dokurno and use cream. Sherry, curry, and mustard lend perfect flavor balance to the rich sauce.

Add flour to melted butter and cook 3 minutes. Add hot milk and warm cream and cook until smooth. Add all other ingredients except crabmeat and cook 5 minutes. Add crabmeat and simmer.

As a main course, divide into 6 casseroles and sprinkle each with Parmesan cheese. Bake 15 to 20 minutes in a 350-degree oven.

As an appetizer, divide into clean clam or oyster shells. Sprinkle with Parmesan cheese and bake 8 to 10 minutes in a 350-degree oven.

Fried Fish Batter

2 cups flour

2 eggs, beaten

1 package dry yeast, dissolved in

    ¼ cup warm water

1 can beer

Is there any question about the consistency of a batter made with yeast and beer? It is guaranteed to be light and crispy. Just remember to have the fish dry so the batter will adhere and be sure the oil is hot enough to brown the batter. How hot? Really hot. If you can find a thermometer, do what it says for fried fish.

Mix all ingredients and let stand at room temperature for 2 hours before using. Leftover batter can be covered and kept refrigerated for about 3 weeks.

Halibut and Spinach

Serves 4

1 onion, sliced thin and halved

1 tablespoon butter

4 halibut steaks, 4 to 6 ounces each

Salt, pepper, and dill weed

1 quart packed spinach leaves

1 teaspoon lemon juice or vinegar

Crumbled egg garnish, if desired

Students of the microwave oven praise its efficiency for fish cookery. Halibut steaks are no exception. When the micro-cooked steaks are served on spinach, half of the dinner is prepared. Add a salad. It's completed.

Place onion and butter on large microwave-safe serving platter. Cover with plastic wrap. Microcook on high 3 minutes or until onion is tender; turn dish 1/4 turn once during cooking.

Season halibut with salt, pepper, and dill. Place in a second microwave-safe dish, cover with plastic wrap. Cook on medium (50% power) 6 to 7 minutes or until fish flakes when tested with a fork; turn dish 1/4 turn once during cooking. Keep warm.

Place spinach leaves with water clinging to them over onion mixture. Microcook, covered, on high 2 minutes, until spinach is wilted. Sprinkle with salt and pepper; stir. Place cooked halibut on spinach mixture. Spoon 1/4 of the crumbled egg garnish over each serving.

CRUMBLED EGG GARNISH: Chop 1 hard cooked egg and work 1 tablespoon firm butter and 1/4 teaspoon dill weed into it with fork until crumbly. Makes about 1/3 cup.

Linguini with White Clam Sauce

Serves 2

2 tablespoons olive oil

1 large garlic clove, minced

1 small onion, finely chopped

1 (10-ounce) can whole baby clams

1/4 cup chopped parsley

1 tablespoon lemon juice

12 ounces linguine, cooked

Shredded Parmesan cheese

A well-stocked pantry is insurance for quick meals. Dinner is just a few minutes away when linguini and canned clams are on hand. It doesn't take much longer to prepare the sauce than it does to cook the pasta.

Heat oil in medium skillet. Sauté garlic and onion until soft, not browned. Add clams, parsley, and lemon juice. Heat.

Serve over hot, cooked linguine. Sprinkle with Parmesan cheese.

Nasi Goreng

Serves 4

¼ cup butter

2 tablespoons curry powder

1 cup uncooked rice

Salt and pepper

1 cup, or more, chicken broth

1 cup chopped, parboiled or partly
cooked celery and onion

1 cup shrimp, peeled and cleaned

½ cup diced ham, veal, chicken livers,
or tiny meatballs

Cucumber, peeled and sliced lengthwise, or a fried egg for each
portion as garnish

A Javanese entree that takes well to any or all leftover meat or poultry, this is a colorful dish. Warning! Two tablespoons of curry may be excessive for some tender palates.

Melt butter. Add curry powder and stir until it is a smooth blend. Add rice and stir again until each grain is coated and covered. Add salt, pepper, and chicken broth. Cover and transfer to 325-degree oven. Cook until rice is tender and flaky, about 25 minutes.

Add celery and onion, shrimp, and bits of meat. Heat just long enough to get really hot. Top each serving with sliced cucumber or fried egg.

Poached Salmon with Curry Sauce

Serves 4

4 salmon fillets

Salt and pepper

3 tablespoons melted butter

Curry Sauce:

3 onions, minced

3 parsley sprigs

1 sprig fresh thyme, or
   use 1/2 teaspoon dried

1 bay leaf

3 tablespoons butter

2 grinds of freshly grated nutmeg

2 rounded tablespoons flour

1 teaspoon curry powder

2 cups heated chicken broth

2 cups half and half, or milk

Irene Kaufman's recipe is a lesson in fish cookery. The former cooking school director tells us how to poach salmon and how to make a sauce that is suitable for many kinds of fish. Now a full-time caterer, she is known for artistic food designs. As she says, "I don't do dips."

Cook onions, parsley, thyme, and bay leaf in covered skillet for 5 minutes; stir occasionally until soft. Add grated nutmeg. Stir in flour; cook a few minutes without browning. Add curry powder. Remove from heat; whisk in broth. Simmer, uncovered, over low heat for 1 hour, stirring often.

Strain sauce through fine wire sieve into heavy saucepan. Beat in cream with whisk. Keep warm over very low heat while preparing salmon.

Butter skillet. Season salmon fillets with salt and pepper. Put in pan; drizzle 3 tablespoons of melted butter over them. Lay sheet of waxed paper over salmon and cover tightly with a lid. Poach fish in butter and steam over low heat. Turn once. Total cooking time is 10 to 12 minutes.

To serve, arrange salmon on heated serving dish; spoon half the sauce around it. Serve remaining sauce in a sauceboat.

Shrimp Creole in Rice Ring

Serves 8 to 10

2 medium onions, finely chopped

1 clove garlic, finely chopped

2 large green peppers, coarsely chopped

1 cup chopped celery

¼ cup bacon drippings

1 (20-ounce) can tomatoes

1 (6-ounce) can tomato paste

¼ cup finely chopped parsley

2 teaspoons salt

1 teaspoon paprika

¼ teaspoon pepper

1 (10-ounce) package frozen, cut okra,
   thawed and drained

2 pounds large shrimp, shelled and deveined

1 teaspoon gumbo filé

Saffron rice ring

This recipe is dated 1965, long before southern Louisiana Cajun and Creole cooking styles were copied from coast to coast. The pink shrimp that simmers with okra and green pepper before being spooned into a rice ring, yellow with saffron, makes an attractive dinner entree. Hosts who want to complete the Louisiana theme serve bread pudding with whiskey sauce for dessert.

Sauté onions, garlic, peppers, and celery in hot bacon drippings until tender, stirring occasionally. Add tomatoes, tomato paste, and parsley; simmer 30 to 45 minutes, stirring occasionally, until thick. Season with salt, paprika, and pepper.
Add okra; cover and cook 10 minutes; add shrimp, cover and cook 5 minutes longer. Stir in gumbo filé; immediately spoon into center of saffron rice ring.

SAFFRON RICE RING; Bring 4 cups chicken stock to a boil; add ¼ teaspoon saffron, crumbled, 2 cups long grain raw rice, salt, and 3 tablespoons butter. Cover tightly and cook over low heat 20 to 25 minutes, until rice is tender and water is absorbed. Spoon into 6-cup buttered ring mold; pack lightly. Let stand 5 minutes; unmold on heated serving platter.

Shrimp Curry in a Hurry

Serves 4

1/4 cup butter

1 large onion, chopped

3 tablespoons flour

1 cup applesauce

1 can condensed beef bouillon

1 1/2 teaspoons curry powder

1/4 teaspoon ground ginger

1/4 teaspoon salt

Ground red pepper

2 1/2 tablespoons lemon juice

10 ounces frozen shrimp, or

    1 1/2 cups fresh

3 cups cooked rice

Applesauce is the surprise sweetness in this working person's shrimp entree, but curry powder, ginger, ground red pepper, and lemon juice jump in quickly for balance.

In large skillet, melt butter and add chopped onion. Cook until tender, about 5 minutes. Stir in flour. Add applesauce, beef bouillon, curry powder, ginger, salt, dash of ground red pepper, and lemon juice. Blend well.

Thaw, remove shells, and clean shrimp. Add shrimp; simmer, uncovered, about 5 minutes until shrimp are tender and sauce is thickened. Serve over cooked rice.

Sister City Paella

1 cup dry white wine
1 tablespoon red wine vinegar
2 cups each: chicken broth and
    beef bouillon
1/4 teaspoon saffron threads
1 teaspoon paprika
1/4 teaspoon each: ground red pepper
    and oregano
1/2 teaspoon thyme
2 garlic cloves, pressed
Salt and pepper
1 large onion, sliced
2 medium red peppers, sliced
2 tablespoons olive oil
10 chicken thighs
1/2 cup vegetable oil
2 cups raw rice
1 cup pitted ripe olives
1 (10-ounce) package each: frozen peas
    and artichoke hearts
1 large tomato, peeled, seeded,
    and cut into wedges
1/2 pound each: ham and cooked chorizo,
    each cut into 10 pieces
1 pound cooked large shrimp
20 clams, steamed and open
1/2 cup toasted almonds
1 tablespoon capers
Chopped parsley for garnish

When visitors from Toledo, Spain are served their national dish in their sister city in Ohio, they praise the cook and clean up their plates. With chicken, shrimp, ham, and sausage on saffron rice, this is an ideal dish for a crowd because there is something for everyone.

Combine all ingredients from white wine through salt and pepper to make sauce base.

Sauté onions and peppers in olive oil. Brown chicken thighs in vegetable oil. Drain off fat; add sautéed onions and peppers and sauce base.

Twenty minutes before serving, sprinkle raw rice into sauce mix gently. Let boil rapidly 5 to 6 minutes, but do not cover pan or stir the rice; mix down only.

Sprinkle with all other ingredients to arrange attractively and simmer 10 minutes.

Sole Amandine

2 tablespoons butter

2 tablespoons oil

1½ pounds fresh sole fillets

Milk

¼ cup sliced almonds

Juice of 1 lemon

¾ cup Chablis wine

½ cup V-8 juice, to which ¼ cup
     water has been added

Butter, lemon juice, and white wine—there's nothing unusual about cooking fish with all three. This is just a reminder of how special it can be.

Heat butter and oil in sauté pan. Dip fish in milk; dust with flour. Sauté fish until browned on both sides.

Remove from pan. Add almonds and additional butter, if needed; sauté until light brown. Add lemon juice, Chablis, and diluted juice to pan. Simmer until liquid is reduced by ⅓; pour over fish and serve.

Sole with Zucchini Basil Sauté

1½ pounds sole fillets

¼ cup dry vermouth

¼ cup water

1 tablespoon lemon juice

2 tablespoons chopped shallots

½ cup coarsely grated zucchini,
    not peeled

3 tablespoons coarsely grated carrots

¼ teaspoon basil

3 tablespoons low-fat cream cheese

Salt and pepper

A three-vegetable, low-fat cream cheese sauce is more than just healthful. It's colorful, with zucchini and carrots.

Rinse fish with cold water; pat dry with paper towels. Pour vermouth, water, and lemon juice into a large, non-stick skillet. Bring to a boil; reduce heat. Arrange fish in a single layer in skillet. Cover and simmer 3 to 5 minutes, or until fish just turns opaque. Transfer to warm serving platter. Reserve cooking liquid.

Simmer to reduce cooking liquid by half. Add shallots, zucchini, carrots, and basil. Cook and stir just until limp.

Stir in cream cheese until mixture is smooth and thickened. Pour off any accumulated juice on bottom of serving platter. Season fish with salt and pepper. Pour vegetable mixture over fish and serve immediately.

Green Bean and Lamb Stew

Serves 6 to 8

2 pounds lamb meat, cut into cubes

2 tablespoons butter

2 cups water

Salt

1 onion, diced

3 (20-ounce) cans green beans,
    drained

1 can tomato paste

Pinch allspice

Pinch cinnamon

Black pepper

Allspice and cinnamon are essential seasonings in a Middle Eastern lamb stew, which makes excellent family fare on a cold night.

Brown lamb in butter just until brown; add water and season with salt. Cook over low heat; add more water if necessary. Add onion and beans; cook 10 minutes more, covered.

Dilute tomato paste with a little water and add it to the meat-bean mixture. Add enough water to cover. Add allspice, cinnamon, and pepper. Cook, covered, over low heat until meat is tender, about a half hour.

Lamb with Couscous

Serves 6

1½ pounds lean, boneless lamb shoulder,

   cut into 1-inch cubes

1 tablespoon vegetable oil

¾ cup chopped onions

2 garlic cloves, minced

1 tablespoon dried tarragon leaves,

   crushed

1½ cups tomato juice

1 medium green pepper, cut into strips

¾ cup dried apricots, quartered

1 cup couscous

Additional dried apricots and

   fresh tarragon, for garnish

Tarragon, an herb that is particularly complimentary to meats, and sweet, dried apricots have a dual role here. They season lamb as it cooks and also garnish the platter when it is assembled with couscous.

In a large skillet, brown lamb in oil. Add onions, garlic, and tarragon; cook until onions are tender-crisp. Drain off fat. Stir in tomato juice, green pepper, and apricots. Cover and simmer 15 to 20 minutes, or until lamb is cooked.

Prepare couscous as package directs, using only 1 tablespoon butter. Fluff lightly with a fork; spoon onto platter. Top with lamb mixture. Garnish with additional apricots and tarragon.

Marinated Shish Kabobs

Serves 6

2 pounds boneless lamb, preferably

    cut from the leg, in 2-inch cubes

½ cup fresh lemon juice

½ cup olive oil

1 teaspoon salt

½ teaspoon crumbled oregano

1 large onion, sliced into thin rounds

3 large garlic cloves, peeled

    and smashed

2 tablespoons chopped parsley

15 to 20 bay leaves

Think about this combination in marinade: olive oil, garlic, lemon juice, and oregano. Can't you almost smell the lamb kabobs sizzling on the grill? It is a winning Middle Eastern formula that also can be used to season chicken.

Trim and cut lamb. Beat lemon juice with olive oil, salt, and oregano. Add lamb and other ingredients to dish. Toss to moisten lamb well. Marinate, refrigerated, at least 6 hours.

Put bay leaf between each piece of lamb on skewer. If the meat fits tightly, it will char on the outside and be rare inside.

Grill over charcoal or broil indoors. Cook 3 inches from the heat for at least 10 minutes and turn while cooking.

Fruit-Rice Stuffed Crown Roast of Pork

Serves 12

1 (8-pound) crown pork roast, or 12 ribs
Lemon juice
Salt and pepper
1/2 cup Dijon mustard
2 tablespoons soy sauce
1 garlic clove, minced
1 teaspoon sage
1/4 teaspoon marjoram
Fruit stuffing:
2 tablespoons butter
1 medium onion, chopped
1 cup each: chopped celery
    and bread crumbs
2 cups cooked rice
1/2 teaspoon each: marjoram
    and thyme
1 teaspoon sage
Salt and pepper
1 large can pineapple tidbits, drained
1 cup each: fresh orange sections
    and golden raisins
1/4 cup blanched, slivered almonds,
    if desired
1/2 cup dry white wine

The crown of pork picks up the tantalizing flavors of soy, sage, and mustard before it is stuffed with a pineapple-raisin stuffing in a smashing presentation worthy of an elegant dinner party for 8 to 10 guests.

Rub roast inside and out with lemon juice and season with salt and pepper. Fill cavity with crumbled aluminum foil to retain shape. Roast, uncovered, 1 hour in 325-degree oven.

Combine mustard, soy sauce, garlic, sage, and marjoram; rub inside and outside of roast; return to bake 1 hour. Remove foil.

Sauté onion and celery in butter. Stir in rice and seasonings. Add remaining ingredients: mix well. Pack dressing into roast cavity; cover with foil. Roast 1 more hour, until meat thermometer registers 170 degrees. Decorate bone tips with kumquats or paper frills.

photo on cover

Pork Loin with Apples and Prunes

Serves 6

1 tablespoon flour

1 (4 to 4 ½ -pound) center loin

    pork roast

12 pitted prunes

12 to 18 thin tart apple wedges,

    not peeled

2 teaspoons soy sauce

¼ cup dark brown sugar,

    firmly packed

1 teaspoon ginger

½ teaspoon garlic salt, if desired

¼ teaspoon pepper

The appearance, the taste, the texture. Each is equally outstanding. The loin gets a soy-ginger rub down. Apples and prunes hide during baking but make an impressive showing when the meat is sliced.

Sprinkle flour into a large oven cooking bag and place in baking dish. Turn roast rib side down and make 6 pockets by cutting slits in meaty side of roast, deep enough to hold prunes and apples but shallow enough to let them show a little. Place 2 prunes and 2 or 3 apple slices in each pocket. Brush roast with soy sauce.

Combine brown sugar, ginger, garlic salt, and pepper and rub over top and sides of roast. Or add the soy sauce to the dry seasonings to make a paste and rub over roast.

Place roast, rib side down, in cooking bag and close with tie. Make 6 slits in bag. Bake in 325-degree oven for 2½ to 3 hours until a meat thermometer registers 170 degrees.

Upside Down Candied Ham Loaf

Serves 10 to 12

2 cups whole wheat bread crumbs

1 cup milk

2 eggs, slightly beaten

2 pounds ground ham

1 pound lean ground beef

1 teaspoon dry mustard

½ teaspoon salt

½ cup brown sugar

½ teaspoon ground cloves

Surprise. Surprise. A ham loaf that isn't topped with pineapple slices and maraschino cherries. Here is a simple, basic recipe that includes ground beef. Save the pineapple for a salad.

Soak bread crumbs in milk. Add eggs. Thoroughly combine ground ham, beef, mustard, salt, and bread and milk mixture. Mix well.

Combine brown sugar and cloves and spread on bottom of 5-by-9-inch loaf pan. Form meat mixture into loaf and place in pan. Bake 1½ hours in 350-degree oven. Invert onto serving platter.

Lemon Herb Turkey Breast

1 (4 to 6-pound) turkey breast

2 sprigs each, fresh sage, rosemary,
    oregano, basil, and thyme

4 to 6 sprigs fresh parsley

1 lemon

Fresh herbs form a beautiful green pattern as they bake under the skin in this low fat recipe, which can be adapted for a whole turkey or chicken. It takes courage to pull the skin up to arrange the herb bouquet and then replace it, but the technique works.

Wash and dry herbs and parsley and divide into two bundles; save any extra herbs to use later.

Loosen skin on both sides of turkey breast with a sharp-pointed knife. The skin can be further loosened by carefully pushing between it and the flesh with a case knife or other thin, blunt instrument. It will loosen fairly easily. Be careful not to poke a hole in it. The skin must remain connected to the breast bone. Tuck each bundle of fresh herbs on either side of the breast. Spread around with fingers or with the case knife to distribute evenly.

Using a fork, deeply pierce the whole lemon several times and place it in the breast cavity. Place the prepared turkey breast, bone side up, on a meat rack in a shallow roasting pan. Bake in 325-degree oven until it reaches 170 degrees on a meat thermometer. Let turkey breast stand 10 minutes before slicing.

Serve each portion with a sprig of fresh herbs.

Wild Rice Stuffing for Turkey

Yields enough for a very large bird

½ pound sausage

¾ pound butter

3 cups chopped onion

6 cups chopped celery

2 pounds dried bread cubes

2 cups cooked wild rice

2 teaspoons poultry seasoning

3 tablespoons chopped parsley

3 eggs, beaten

½ gallon chicken stock, homemade
    or canned

It was a lucky day for Anne Sickelbaugh when she found the family's turkey stuffing recipe tucked in an old cookbook after her mother's death. The young woman said it just wouldn't be Thanksgiving without this recipe. The dressing is fluffy with eggs and has a pleasant rice texture. It won the stuffing category in The Blade's 1993 Thanksgiving Menu Contest.

(Note: If stuffing is to be cooked in a casserole and not in the turkey, use only ½ pound butter.)

Crumble and brown sausage over medium heat in Dutch oven. Add 1 cup butter and stir until it melts. Add onions and celery and continue to cook until celery is tender-crisp and onions are transparent. Transfer to large bowl and add bread cubes, cooked wild rice, poultry seasoning, parsley, and beaten eggs.

Soften last ¼ pound butter and work into stuffing with clean hands. Pour half of stock over stuffing. Let it be absorbed in the dressing before adding about half of the rest of the stock; use more if dressing seems dry. Mix to fluff and blend.

Stuff prepared turkey and bake according to turkey weight. Spoon excess stuffing into a greased casserole and bake the last hour the turkey is baking.

Turkey Oscar

2 tablespoons butter

4 fresh turkey breast slices

1 can asparagus tips, drained, or use
   fresh, if available, cooked just
   until done

1 can crabmeat, drained

Hollandaise sauce (below)

Forget the veal and bring out this economical, low fat turkey which is made like the original Oscar, with asparagus, crabmeat, and hollandaise. The blender hollandaise recipe is a bonus.

Melt 1 tablespoon butter in skillet on medium. When butter begins to brown, add turkey. Cook 5 minutes, turn. Top each with asparagus and crabmeat. Cover. Cook 2 more minutes.
Place on platter and keep warm. Top with warm hollandaise sauce.

HOLLANDAISE SAUCE: In a blender, place 3 egg yolks, 2 tablespoons lemon juice, ½ teaspoon salt, and a pinch of ground red pepper or hot pepper sauce. Melt ½ cup butter and slowly pour it into blender while it is running on low speed.

Sweetbreads en Brochette

Serves 4

1 pound veal sweetbreads

1/2 cup lemon juice

1 teaspoon Worcestershire sauce

1 teaspoon salt

1/2 teaspoon pepper

1/2 teaspoon dry mustard

24 mushroom caps

12 bacon slices, cut in halves

1/2 cup melted butter

Chopped parsley

Skewered sweetbreads, bacon rolls, and mushroom caps cooked on the outdoor grill are sure to bring compliments to the amateur chef in the house. It surely did for the man who won $10,000 with this recipe at the 1963 Hawaii Open for Outdoor Chefs.

Simmer sweetbreads in boiling salted water, covered, 25 minutes. Drain and place in cold water; remove membranes and veins. Cut into 24 pieces, cover and refrigerate overnight, or at least several hours.

Combine lemon juice, Worcestershire sauce, salt, pepper, and mustard. Pour over the mushroom caps in a bowl. Refrigerate; toss occasionally.

Preheat barbecue grill until coals are covered with ash, and heat is very hot and steady. Roll up bacon pieces and string on skewers, alternating with sweetbread pieces and mushroom caps.

Grill 15 to 20 minutes, turning often and brushing with butter. Place on warm platter; pour remaining butter over all and sprinkle with parsley.

Veal Piccata

1½ pounds veal scallops,

    cut ¼-inch thick

½ cup flour

½ teaspoon salt

Pepper to taste

3 tablespoons oil

1 garlic clove

3 tablespoons lemon juice

¼ cup dry white wine

    (more as needed)

2 tablespoons chopped fresh parsley

12 very thin lemon slices

This Italian classic cooks quickly and is light and vibrant with a white wine and lemon sauce. Pasta is an appropriate accompaniment.

Pound veal between two pieces of waxed paper. Dredge veal in flour to which salt and pepper have been added. Heat oil quite hot. Brown garlic in oil and remove. Brown floured veal scallops one minute on each side and remove to serving platter and keep warm.

Add lemon and white wine to make a sauce, scraping meat particles into sauce to help thicken it. Spoon over meat on platter. Garnish with parsley and lemon slices.

Lentil-Brown Rice Stew

Serves 8

2 tablespoons olive oil

3 large garlic cloves, minced

3 cups coarsely chopped onion

3 celery ribs, sliced

2½ cups brown rice, picked over,
   and rinsed

¾ cup dried lentils, picked over,
   and rinsed

½ pound mushrooms, sliced

4¾ cups chicken, or vegetable,
   stock or bouillon

2 bay leaves

1 ½ teaspoons dried oregano

1 tablespoon prepared mustard

½ teaspoon salt, or to taste

1 cup tomato sauce

1 cup minced parsley, less if preferred

The microwave oven isn't the only appliance that shortens cooking time. The pressure cooker also is in the fast food lane and is making a comeback, particularly for dried legumes and grains. Here lentils and brown rice cook to tenderness under pressure and pick up the pungency of bay leaves and oregano.

Heat oil in pressure cooker. Sauté garlic and onions until browned. Stir in celery, brown rice, and lentils. Sauté another minute. Add mushrooms, stock, bay leaves, oregano, and mustard. Bring to a boil.

Lock lid in place over high heat and bring to high pressure. Adjust heat to maintain high pressure and cook for 20 minutes. Let pressure drop naturally for 10 minutes. Release any remaining pressure. Remove lid, tilting it away from you to allow steam to escape.

Remove bay leaves and stir in salt, tomato sauce, and parsley. If rice or lentils are not quite done, cover and simmer over low heat until desired consistency, stirring in a little boiling water if it seems too dry.

Zucchini Spaghetti Sauce

Serves 6

1½ pounds mild Italian sausage, cut into

    small pieces (or use smoked sausage)

4 ounces fresh mushrooms, sliced

½ cup cooking sherry

3 chicken bouillon cubes

1½ pounds zucchini, sliced and not pared

1 (4-ounce) jar pimientos,

    drained and chopped

¼ cup chopped onion

1 (15-ounce) can marinara

    spaghetti sauce

½ cup water

In 1977 thousands of copies of this recipe were distributed to women's organizations with a reminder, "Zucchini is like sincere friendship. It just grows and grows."

Brown sausage and mushrooms. Add sherry and bouillon cubes; stir until cubes dissolve. Add zucchini slices, pimiento, and onion. Cook, uncovered, until zucchini is soft and sausage is done, about 30 minutes. Add canned marinara sauce and water. Cook 15 minutes more. Serve with cooked spaghetti.

Accompaniments

Accompaniments balance the menu. They are the "go with" foods; the vegetables, fruits, and the grains. Accompaniments are the part of the meal that is seasonal, healthful, and usually less costly than the main dish.

In grandmother's day these same foods were called side dishes, and in restaurants with blue plate specials, two side dishes are often included.

Today the term does not apply. Sides have moved center stage and are considered a more valuable contribution to health than the main dish. Two vegetables are better than one at mealtimes, the experts say, and five fruits and vegetables a day are recommended to ward off serious illness.

Ohio farmers provide an abundance of produce. Roadside stands showcase home-grown fruits and vegetables, beginning with spring asparagus and ending with apples and squash in the fall. Home canning and freezing are still a way of life to preserve the local harvest for winter.

Tomatoes and corn, major Ohio crops, star in two heirloom accompaniments. Tomato pudding, a buttery rich pudding, is claimed as an original and is usually served to out of town guests as a symbol of local hospitality. Edna Crisman's Corn Fritters that rise golden and fluffy from the fryer are legendary in this region. Fact is, a true northwest Ohio menu should include both the tomato pudding and the golden fritters.

On opposite page: Ohio tomatoes are twice as good eating with Tabbouleh, chèvre cheese, and bulgur stuffings and toppings. (page 135-136)

Asparagus Roll-Ups

1 (8-ounce) package cream cheese

½ cup grated Parmesan cheese

1 loaf white sandwich bread,

    crusts removed

1 pound, or more, asparagus spears

1 cup butter, melted

Sesame seeds

Hot, crispy bread rolls, filled and baked with asparagus and cheese, can be cut small into bite-size appetizers or served full-sized with a salad.

Mix cream cheese and half the Parmesan cheese. Melt butter. Roll out bread flat on each side. Spread one side of bread with cheese mixture to cover.

Place an asparagus spear diagonally on cheese and roll up with the cheese and asparagus inside. Dip roll into melted butter.

Place seam side down in buttered 9-by-13-inch pan. Repeat until bread and asparagus are used. Drizzle any remaining butter over roll-ups and sprinkle with remaining Parmesan cheese and sesame seeds.

Bake about 40 minutes in preheated 325-degree oven, until golden and puffy.

Slow-Cooker Apple Butter

10 pounds cooking apples

4 cups apple cider

Sugar

Cinnamon, cloves, allspice, and nutmeg

The aroma of apples, cider, and spices is so tantalizing that everyone wants to dip into this hot butter the minute it is done.

Wash apples but do not pare. Quarter and remove seeds. Add cider and cook slowly until soft. Put through food mill or sieve.

Measure pulp. For each 3 cups of pulp, add 1 cup sugar, 1 tablespoon cinnamon, ½ teaspoon cloves, ½ teaspoon allspice, and ½ teaspoon nutmeg.

Put in slow cooker and cook on low about 18 hours, until the mixture is as thick and dark as desired.

Pour into sterilized pint jars. The butter can be processed in a boiling water bath 10 minutes or frozen.

Lima Beans with Sour Cream

Serves 8 to 10

1 pound dry baby limas

1/4 pound butter

1/2 cup brown sugar

1 tablespoon salad mustard

2 tablespoons molasses

1 cup sour cream

It's the old flavoring team of brown sugar, mustard, and molasses to season baked beans, but this time the beans are limas, and sour cream is added. This is an excellent side dish, particularly with ham. Just don't try the sour cream trick with Boston beans.

Soak beans in water overnight. The next day cook beans in water until nearly done. Mix in butter. Combine brown sugar, salad mustard, and molasses and add to beans. Fold in sour cream.

Bake in greased casserole 45 minutes in 350-degree oven.

Old-Fashioned Harvard Beets

8 medium beets

2 tablespoons butter

1 tablespoon flour

2 whole cloves

½ cup sugar

⅓ cup lemon juice

Salt and pepper

The educated beets that carry the Harvard name are simmered in a sweet-sour sauce. Could it be that they were first served in the Harvard University dining hall? If you must, use canned beets.

Boil beets in skins until tender; slip off skins. Slice or dice.
Melt butter in saucepan; add flour and stir. Add cloves, sugar, and lemon juice. Stir and cook until transparent before adding beets. Season to taste with salt and pepper.

Cabbage Pancakes

6 cups shredded green cabbage

2 eggs

1 egg yolk

1/2 cup milk

1 cup all-purpose flour

3 tablespoons butter, melted

1/2 teaspoon salt

1 1/2 tablespoons chopped
   green onion tops

2 to 3 tablespoons more butter

There seems to be a lot of cabbage in this book, which shows not only a personal preference of the food editor, but the vegetable's versatility. We couldn't bear to overlook these crisp vegetable pancakes with just the right amount of onion. They are fried in small circles and are delicious with duck or pork.

Cook cabbage, covered, in a little boiling salted water 5 minutes. Rinse under cold running water until cool; drain very well. Wrap cabbage in paper towel and squeeze out all liquid. Place cabbage in large bowl.

Combine eggs, egg yolk, milk, flour, butter, and salt in that order in a blender container. Blend until smooth. Combine with cabbage in bowl. Stir in onion tops.

Melt 1 tablespoon butter in large heavy skillet over medium heat. Spoon 1 tablespoon of batter into skillet at a time. Cook 3 or 4 at a time, depending on the size of the skillet, until golden brown on each side. Keep warm in oven. More butter may have to be added as the batter is cooked.

Edna Crisman's Corn Fritters

Yields 12 to 15

3 eggs, separated

1 (1-pound) can yellow cream-style corn

2 cups flour

2 tablespoons baking powder

2 tablespoons sugar

Pinch salt

Oil or solid vegetable shortening for frying

Edna Crisman, who for many years operated the Hostess House for private parties in Delta, Ohio, was known for setting a fine table and serving excellent home-style foods, including fried chicken. But the recipe everyone wanted was for the corn fritters that bubbled to a beautiful golden brown and were as tender as love. The recipe remained a secret until after her death at the age of 103. In her will she bequeathed the recipe to The Blade food editor to publish for the people of northwest Ohio. This is one of the greatest compliments a food editor could receive.

Beat egg yolks and stir into corn. Combine flour, baking powder, sugar, and salt. Stir into egg yolk-corn mixture and mix well. Beat egg whites stiff and fold into batter. Mix egg whites into batter thoroughly, but with gentle motions. A wooden spoon works well.

In the meantime, heat shortening to 350 degrees. Using a large round soup spoon, drop spoonfuls of fritter batter into hot fat. Make one or more at a time, depending upon the amount of oil used. The fritters will quickly come to the surface. Let each one cook a little; then turn it over until the entire fritter is lightly browned and crisp.

Cooking time is no more than 3 minutes, possibly less. It depends upon the amount of batter dropped into the oil.

Remove with a slotted spoon and drain on paper towels. Serve with butter and maple syrup. Can be kept warm in low temperature oven.

Frosted Cauliflower

1 medium head cauliflower

1/2 cup mayonnaise

1/4 teaspoon salt

1 to 2 teaspoons prepared mustard

3/4 cup shredded sharp

    Cheddar cheese

Paprika, if desired

When microwave ovens were new and fascinating in the late 60s and early 70s, salespeople had a few standard items they demonstrated to prove the wonders of the new appliance. One popular demo was baked potatoes. Other prospective buyers watched hot dogs and bacon cook in paper towels, and the more advanced sales force made frosted cauliflower and passed out samples. The idea boosted cauliflower sales as well as microwave business.

Remove woody base from cauliflower. Leave whole and place in 1½-quart casserole to which 2 tablespoons water have been added. Cook 6 to 7 minutes in microwave.

Combine mayonnaise, salt, and mustard; microwave 1 minute. Spread on cauliflower. Sprinkle with grated cheese, which will melt on the hot cauliflower. Sprinkle with paprika, if desired.

Red Cabbage with Apples and Red Wine

Serves 8

1 tart apple, peeled, cored, and sliced

1 large onion, chopped

1/4 cup bacon fat, or oil

3 peppercorns

1 head red cabbage, finely sliced

1/2 cup red wine

1 medium onion

1 bay leaf, broken

1 whole clove

Salt and pepper

Here's one of the best answers on what to do with a head of red cabbage. Peppercorns, red wine, and bay leaves are flavor mates that make it compatible with pork and veal. Sliced apples round out the flavor.

Sauté apples and onions in bacon fat until golden. Add cabbage and peppercorns and sauté for 5 minutes.

Deglaze with red wine. Add medium onion, which has been studded with bay leaf and clove. Season with salt and pepper. Simmer 1/2 hour. Remove onion with bay leaf and clove before serving.

Toasted Cabbage and Noodles

Serves 4

1 small head cabbage

½ cup butter

1 large onion, chopped

1 garlic clove, minced or pressed

2 tablespoons sugar

8 ounces wide egg noodles

Salt and pepper

Immigrants who settled in Toledo in the late 1800s to work in the glass factories and in other industries brought wonderful Old World dishes such as this one, which is low in cost but high in flavor.

Finely shred cabbage and discard core. It should make 6 to 8 cups. Melt butter in wide frying pan over medium heat. Add onion and garlic and cook and stir until onion is soft. Add cabbage and cook and continue to stir until cabbage is limp and turns a brighter green, about 5 minutes.

Sprinkle with sugar and continue to cook and stir often until cabbage takes on an amber color and begins to brown lightly, which will take another 25 minutes.

Meanwhile cook noodles al dente. Drain. In a shallow bowl, combine noodles and cabbage mixture. Lift with 2 forks to mix well. Season to taste with salt and pepper.

Eggplant Parmigiana

Serves 6

1 large eggplant

Salt and pepper

1 cup fine bread crumbs

2 eggs, lightly beaten

Olive oil

1½ cups tomato sauce, heated

½ pound mozzarella cheese, sliced

1 teaspoon dried basil, crumbled

¼ cup Parmesan cheese, grated

The trend, at least at this writing, but things change fast in the food world, is for an increasing number of Americans to eat meatless meals two or three times a week. It isn't necessary for them to search for a substitute. Some of the old classics, like this Italian eggplant and cheese standby, are getting attention as meatless alternatives. The appropriate companion dish is pasta.

Wash eggplant and trim ends. Cut crosswise into ¼-inch thick slices, or thicker. Do not peel. Season with salt and pepper, then dip into bread crumbs, dip into egg, and then dip into bread crumbs again. Refrigerate for 30 minutes.

Heat about ⅛ inch oil in skillet. Fry eggplant slices until tender and golden on both sides. Add more oil when necessary. Drain on absorbent paper.

Line a buttered, shallow baking dish with some of the sauce. Add a sprinkling of basil and Parmesan. Repeat layers until dish is full.

Bake in a preheated 350-degree oven for 25 to 30 minutes.

Cheese Grits

Serves 6

½ cup regular grits

2 cups water

½ teaspoon salt

¼ cup butter or shortening

1 roll garlic-flavored processed cheese

1 egg

Milk

Any southern host will attest that grits baked with garlic cheese is the perfect accompaniment to any kind of meat or poultry. It's a definite upgrade from a bowl of grits for breakfast.

Combine grits, water, and salt in saucepan and cook until slightly thickened. Stir in butter and cheese and mix well. Put egg in measuring cup and add enough milk to make ⅔ cup. Beat until frothy. Stir into grits.

Pour into a flat, greased casserole. Bake in 350-degree oven until browned and bubbly on top. Remove from oven and let thicken somewhat before serving.

Pierogi

Filling:

1 small cabbage head

2 cups sauerkraut

1 small onion, chopped

¼ cup butter or shortening

Salt and pepper

Dough:

2 eggs

1½ cups water

1 teaspoon salt

4 cups flour

Butter

Veteran Polish cooks can tell by the feel of the dough when it's ready to be rolled out. Many of the best cooks who have been interviewed in local Polish neighborhoods don't need a recipe or even have one to pass on to their families. But new cooks need specific guidelines to lead them into the Old World art of making these filled dumplings.

Chop cabbage and boil in salted water 5 minutes. Drain and rinse. Drain sauerkraut. Sauté onion in shortening and add cabbage, sauerkraut, salt, and pepper to taste. Let set about 20 minutes to cool and let flavors blend.

To make dough, beat eggs, water, and salt. Add flour, 1 cup at a time. When it thickens, knead on floured board until smooth and elastic. More flour may be needed.

Divide dough into 2 pieces and roll out thin. Cut into large circles with a cookie cutter or glass. Place a spoonful of filling on each circle and brush edges with water. Fold over and press edges together firmly. Press edges with a fork to insure sealing.

Drop into boiling, salted, water and boil 8 to 10 minutes. Drain in colander. Rinse in cold water. Fry in butter and serve hot.

Oprah's Mashed Potatoes

2½ pounds hot cooked pared

    red potatoes

2½ pounds hot cooked pared

    Idaho potatoes

1¼ cups pureed creamed horseradish

10 ounces butter

2 cups heavy cream

Salt and black pepper

Before Oprah Winfrey teamed up with Rosie Daley as her personal chef and threw out the butter and the cream, the television star is said to have enjoyed richly endowed foods such as these mashed potatoes. The recipe is from the Eccentric, a Chicago restaurant with which Oprah is associated.

Whip all ingredients together into somewhat lumpy texture.

Potato Kale Colcannon

7 potatoes, preferably, Yellow Finns

1 large, sweet onion, diced

1 to 2 tablespoons olive oil

4 cups washed, chopped kale

6 garlic cloves, minced

Black pepper

1 tablespoon tamari, or soy sauce

1/4 cup fresh lemon juice

It may come as a surprise to people who push it aside on their dinner plates that kale is a healthful vegetable to be reckoned with. The pretty, ruffled, green, leafy vegetable is a member of the cabbage family and abounds in vitamins A and C. In recent years it has competed with parsley as a garnish, but eat it, it's good for you! Dr. Warren Dick, a professor of foreign languages, has become the official chef for the Phoenix Earth Food Co-op. He developed this recipe for a class at the Seventh Day Adventist Church.

Boil potatoes 15 minutes. Sauté onion in olive oil. Add chopped kale. There should be some water clinging to the kale. Add garlic, pepper, tamari, and lemon juice.

Cover and cook on medium heat until tender and fragrant. Stir occasionally for about 12 minutes. Pare potatoes and mash in large bowl, but leave a few lumps. Add onion-kale mixture and combine with potatoes. If desired, add ½ pound mashed, firm tofu.

Oil casserole dish with olive oil. Turn potato mixture into it. Pat down. Bake in 350-degree oven about 30 minutes, until a golden brown crust forms.

Take to the Reunion Potatoes

1 (32-ounce) package frozen hash brown

   potatoes, thawed

1 pint sour cream

½ cup chopped onions

1 can cream of potato soup

1 can cream of mushroom,

   celery, or chicken soup

10 ounces grated yellow cheese

Salt and pepper

⅓ cup milk

2 cups crushed potato chips

Frozen potatoes and canned soups make quick work of a casserole that serves 16. When it's hot out of the oven, cover this tightly with foil and wrap it in several layers of newspapers to take to the reunion or church supper.

Mix all ingredients but potato chips. Spoon into very lightly buttered casserole dish. Sprinkle with potato chips. Bake 1 hour in 350-degree oven.

Three Cheese Twice-Baked Potatoes

Serves 2

2 large baking potatoes

1 cup low-fat cottage cheese

1/2 cup ricotta cheese, part-skimmed

1/4 cup freshly grated

   parmesan cheese

2 tablespoons fresh parsley

2 tablespoons fresh dill, chopped,

   or 1 tablespoon dried dill weed

Freshly round pepper to taste

What a bargain! The average potato is 100 calories. When we add three kinds of cheese, it's only 156. The potatoes pick up additional personality when fresh herbs are added. Chives, basil, and thyme are recommended, and no one said jalapeño peppers were banned.

Bake potatoes until tender in a 350-degree oven. Cut into halves and scoop out pulp, leaving 1/4-inch shells.

Beat potato pulp with three cheeses, parsley, and fresh herbs, if used. Fill shells with potato-cheese mixture. Return to oven and bake another 15 minutes, until potatoes have brown tinges.

Mashed Rutabagas with Crisp Shallots

Serves 10

2 large rutabagas, about 4 pounds

2 teaspoons salt

1½ cups olive oil

3 tablespoons butter

5 or 6 shallots, peeled and sliced thin,

    or onions

1 cup milk

6 tablespoons butter

½ teaspoon freshly ground black pepper

Rutabagas and other root vegetables are packed with nutrients. Besides, they are good eating. At home we had parsnips at least once a week, and often mother tried to pass off mashed turnips as mashed potatoes. This recipe is an example of the simple treatment root vegetables require. The cooked and mashed rutabagas, sometimes called yellow turnips, are seasoned with sautéed shallots.

Peel rutabagas and cut into 1-inch chunks. Rutabagas take longer to cook than potatoes. Cook with water to cover and 1 teaspoon salt, until tender, about 35 minutes. Drain.

Heat oil with butter over medium heat; add shallots and cook to a rich, golden brown, 30 to 40 minutes. Stir as they cook to brown evenly. Remove shallots from oil and drain on paper towels.

Heat milk and butter over low heat in separate saucepan until butter melts and milk begins to simmer.

Purée rutabagas in several batches in food processor. With motor running, add butter and milk mixture in steady stream and continue to process until the mixture is smooth.

Return to saucepan, season with 1 teaspoon salt and pepper. Reheat and stir over medium heat. Serve hot with shallots sprinkled over the top.

Perrysburg Dinner Party Rice

Serves 6

1 (6-ounce) package long grain

    and wild rice mix

1 cup chopped onion

1 cup chopped celery

3 tablespoons butter

3 tablespoons soy sauce

1 (3-ounce) can sliced mushrooms

1 can water chestnuts, sliced

Long grain and wild rice are dressed for company with vegetables to compliment poultry or meat. It also qualifies as a meatless main dish. Soy sauce, mushrooms, celery, onions, and water chestnuts hold everyone's interest, even the vegetarians.

Cook rice mix according to directions on package. Sauté onion and celery in butter until tender. Mix all ingredients.

Before serving, reheat gently over low heat, stirring often.

Riz (Middle Eastern Rice)

2 cups long-grain rice

6 tablespoons butter

½ cup rosa marina

4 cups hot water

2 teaspoons salt

Rice cooked by the Syrian and Lebanese method is soaked in water and sautéed in butter before it is cooked. The addition of rosa marina, tiny noodle-like pasta, adds interest. This recipe is from the Ladies' Society of St. Elias Orthodox Church.

Wash rice; soak 15 minutes in hot water. Brown rosa marina in melted butter on medium heat. Drain rice and add to butter.

Sauté rice on medium heat; stir occasionally for 5 minutes. Add hot water and salt. Cover; bring to boil. Let boil briskly for 5 minutes. Lower heat to very low; let cook until water is absorbed, about 15 minutes.

Keep covered until ready to serve; then stir well.

All-American Succotash

Serves 6 to 8

2 cups fresh lima beans

2 cups fresh corn

1½ cups water, or more if needed

6 tablespoons butter

Salt

White pepper

Food doesn't get any more American than the combination of lima beans and corn. Native Americans named it succotash and created it from crops growing where the Pilgrims arrived.

Cook limas in boiling, salted water to cover, 18 to 20 minutes, until almost tender. Drain.

Combine corn, limas, and water in saucepan. Bring to a boil and cook, uncovered, over medium heat until corn is tender and water has almost evaporated, 3 minutes. Drain; add butter. Season with salt and white pepper.

Tally Ho Tomato Pudding

1 cup brown sugar

1 cup tomato purée

¼ cup water

2 cups dry bread cubes, crusts removed

½ cup melted butter

Toledo claims this sweet pudding to be its very own and traces it to the Tally Ho Restaurant. It is customary for Toledo hosts to prepare it for out-of-town dinner guests, and the tradition continues at the Columbian House, an 1827 stage coach inn, in Waterville, Ohio. The buttered bread cubes bake through the pudding and turn a golden brown when it is completed. Then it must be served quickly, before it falls.

Combine brown sugar, tomato purée, and water. Cook 5 minutes. While tomato mixture is cooking, put bread cubes in casserole and pour melted butter over. Pour on hot tomato mixture. Do not stir.

Bake 50 minutes in a 325-degree oven. The drier the bread cubes, the more crusty the pudding will be.

Chèvre Tomatoes

4 tomatoes

Salt

Freshly ground black pepper

Pinch dried oregano

Pinch dried basil

8 tablespoons shredded

    chèvre cheese

4 tablespoons bread crumbs

The recipe for these chèvre-topped tomatoes was discovered in a very appropriate location. After taking food editors on a tour of her goat farm in Virginia, the young owner extended hospitality and served the tomatoes topped with her product. Everyone agreed. She does make a chèvre equal to California's, and her presentation of it was equally marketable.

Cut tomatoes in halves. Place, cut side up, on broiler pan or in baking dish. Sprinkle with all other ingredients.

Bake in 300-degree oven or broil 4 inches from heat source until cheese and crumbs begin to form a crust. It will take about 10 minutes if baked, 3 to 4 minutes if broiled.

photo page 112

Stuffed Tomatoes

Spinach:

6 small tomatoes

1 (12 ounce) package spinach soufflé, thawed

½ cup shredded Swiss cheese

⅛ teaspoon ground nutmeg

Bulgar:

8 small tomatoes

Salt

Olive oil

½ cup uncooked bulgar

2 cups tomato juice

½ cup olive oil

1 tablespoon minced garlic

½ teaspoon pepper

Fresh mint

Salt and pepper

2 tablespoons lemon juice

Simple and superb, Ohio-grown tomatoes in season are dressed for dinner with two easy fillings. Spinach soufflé, purchased prepared, is reliably quick and colorful. Bulgar wheat plumps in juices while other foods are cooking.

WITH SPINACH: Cut a star shape from the top of tomatoes and set aside. Scoop out pulp of each tomato, leaving a ¼-inch thick shell. Save pulp for sauces and soups. Place shells in baking pan so they stand close.

Combine spinach soufflé, Swiss cheese, and nutmeg. Spoon into tomato shells. Bake for 20 minutes in 400-degree oven.

Place reserved star tops on tomatoes and continue to bake until filling puffs and is golden, about 10 additional minutes.

WITH BULGAR: Cut thin slices from tomatoes. Scoop out, leaving at least ½-inch shell. Chop flesh and set aside. Sprinkle with salt, prick skin and rub with olive oil. Place cut side down on paper towels to drain. Combine bulgar, tomato juice, olive oil, minced garlic, pepper. Add a little chopped fresh mint if it is available. Let stand 15 minutes, pour into sieve over bowl, let drain 20 minutes. Reserve liquid.

Turn bulgar into clean bowl and add salt and pepper to taste, lemon juice and reserved tomato flesh. Arrange shells, cut side up, around edge of 9-inch pie plate. Mound with bulgar mixture. Pour reserved tomato juice around tomatoes. Cover tightly with plastic wrap and microwave on full power 7 to 9 minutes.

photo page 112

Ratatouille

1/2 cup extra-virgin olive oil

1 medium onion, finely chopped

1 garlic clove, minced

1/2 teaspoon dried leaves of each: basil,

    oregano, thyme, and rosemary

1 pound ripe tomatoes or 1 (20-ounce)

    can tomatoes, chopped with juice

1/4 teaspoon black pepper

1/4 teaspoon ground red pepper

2 medium zucchini, sliced into

    1/4-inch slices, not pared

1 green pepper, seeded and sliced thin

1 red bell pepper, seeded and sliced thin

1 medium eggplant, about 1 pound,

    cut into small cubes

2 tablespoons fresh parsley, minced

While reading through the recipe you can almost smell the onion, garlic, basil, oregano, thyme, and rosemary simmering in olive oil before the vegetables are added. This relish dish, which originated in southern France, is served at room temperature. But heated and spooned over pasta, it is also pretty terrific.

Heat olive oil in large, heavy pot. Sauté onion 3 to 5 minutes until softened. Add garlic, basil, oregano, thyme, and rosemary and sauté briefly. Stir in tomatoes and simmer over low heat, uncovered, 15 minutes. Stir once. Add black and ground red peppers.

Add zucchini, green and fresh red peppers, eggplant, and parsley to sauce. Cover and simmer 30 minutes. Stir once and simmer another 10 minutes. Avoid stirring as much as possible to retain the shape of the vegetables.

Cool in glass or ceramic container overnight. Serve cold, or at room temperature. If desired, garnish with lemon wedges, chopped scallions, Parmesan cheese, and olives. If desired, reheat in covered saucepan over low heat.

NOTE: For color, leave half the eggplant not peeled, but cut unpeeled and peeled portions into uniform cubes.

First Prize Sweet Potato Casserole

Serves 8 to 12

3 cups fresh sweet potatoes,
    cooked and mashed

3/4 cup white sugar

1/2 cup milk

1/2 cup butter, melted

2 eggs, well beaten

1 teaspoon vanilla

Topping:

1 cup brown sugar

1/2 cup flour

1/3 cup milk

1/4 cup butter, melted

1 cup chopped pecans

The food editor's first taste of this holiday casserole is remembered easily. It was at the 1980 Blade Holiday Contest Taste-Off. The taste-offs were always as exciting for her as they were for the finalists who came from all over northwest Ohio bearing the beautiful foods. One spoonful into the sweet potato casserole with the crunchy pecan crust entered by Carol Hartsel, Toledo, and the first prize in vegetables was a sure thing. Please don't consider using canned sweet potatoes here. Only the fresh ones will give the best results.

Combine mashed sweet potatoes with white sugar, milk, first butter, beaten eggs, and vanilla. Pour into buttered baking dish.

Combine topping ingredients and pour over casserole. Bake 30-40 minutes in a 350-degree oven.

Marinated Vegetables

Yields

1 bunch broccoli

1 head cauliflower florets

2 cups diagonally cut carrots,
 ½ -inch thick

1 red pepper, cut into strips

Marinade:

1 large garlic clove, minced

¾ cup vegetable oil

½ to 2 tablespoons red wine vinegar

2 teaspoons sugar

1 teaspoon salt

1 teaspoon dry mustard

1 teaspoon basil

½ teaspoon pepper

⅛ teaspoon nutmeg

Crisp-steamed broccoli, cauliflower, and carrots marinate in a red wine vinaigrette in a recipe that has been kept at the head of the file since it was first tasted by the food editor in Nashville 15 years ago. This vegetable dish is one to stash in the refrigerator to have handy for a late afternoon or evening snack. If you reach for a carrot, you won't reach for a cookie.

Steam vegetables in separate containers until they are tender but not soft. Beat all marinade ingredients and pour over vegetables. Cover and refrigerate.
This will keep for several weeks if tightly covered and refrigerated.

photo on cover

Zucchini and Rice Torta

4 pounds zucchini, sliced thin

4 tablespoons olive oil

2 large onions, chopped fine

4 garlic cloves, mashed

2 cups cooked rice

½ cup Parmesan cheese

3 tablespoons parsley, finely chopped

Salt and pepper to taste

8 eggs, beaten

Four pounds of zucchini? Eight eggs? That's right, and so are the two cups of rice. Put them all together, and it's an Italian casserole which bakes up firm.

Sauté zucchini in 2 tablespoons oil until tender. Pour into large bowl. Sauté onions and garlic in remaining olive oil until soft and golden. Mix onions and zucchini together thoroughly. Add rice, cheese, parsley, salt, and pepper. Mix well.

Pour into 9-by-13-inch oiled glass dish. Bake in preheated 450-degree oven 10 minutes; lower temperature to 350 degrees and bake until firm and golden brown, about 30 minutes longer.

Homemade Noodles

3 egg yolks

1 whole egg

3 tablespoons water

1 teaspoon salt

2 cups flour, or more as needed

The question is, is it necessary to make your own noodles when the supermarket shelves offer a least a dozen different brands? The answer is yes, because none of them has your name on them. This one will.

Beat egg yolks and whole egg until very light. Beat in water and salt. Stir in the flour and work with hands. Divide dough into three parts and roll each out as thin as possible.

When the dough sheets are partially dry, cut into noodles. Separate and let dry completely, or cook immediately.

142

Salads & Dressings

The salad bowl has come of age. It has gained new respect beyond head lettuce with bottled dressing. An extensive variety of greens in the market place invite the serious salad creator to try fascinating combinations of diverse textures and colors, from the chewy arugula and red radicchio, to bronze-tinged leaf lettuce.

Green and crisp, tart or sweet, main dish or side dish, salads are a beautiful mix of fresh produce that set the taste buds in motion.

A saying passed down by the Romans put salads in their place centuries later. "It takes four people to make a salad: a miser to put in vinegar, a spendthrift to add the oil, a wise man to season it, and a mad man to toss it."

All such manner of perfect salad making is represented in this book. The "mad man" in the Roman eulogy to the salad is Bill Zouhary, a gentle, caring soul who taught Toledoans to appreciate the Caesar salad and graciously showed them how to make it. The wise person is the lovely lady, Betty Timko, whose spinach salad and sweet-sour dressing became so popular that she put the dressing on the retail market. The miser is Chef Louis, who uses even the stems of the fresh ingredients in his Spring Salad. The spendthrift? Maybe it is everyone who loves making salads, who puts vegetables, meats, and cheese into the Layered Mexican Cobb Salad.

Name an occasion, and there's a salad candidate. A prize-winning gelatin salad goes to a church supper with style. A couscous salad with tuna is equally fashionable as a luncheon main dish. The traditional Ohio fall salad is apple, preferably with a homemade dressing, and when the occasion is a company dinner, a medley of greens is best dressed with the delectable Wine Cellar's House Mustard Dressing.

On opposite page: Cauliflower with Spinach Dressing is packed with healthful ingredients (page 165).

The Bungalow's French Dressing

Yields about 3 cups

1 can tomato soup

1 cup vinegar

2 teaspoons salt

1/2 teaspoon Worcestershire sauce

1/2 cup salad oil

1/4 cup sugar

1/2 teaspoon pepper

1 teaspoon dry mustard

1 garlic clove, minced

1 teaspoon grated onion

1 teaspoon horseradish

1 teaspoon paprika

Not every restaurant has homemade salad dressings. When you ask for one in most places, the owner hesitates and declines the honor of sharing a secret. Chances are it's because the dressings are commercially bottled, much like those from the grocery stores. But that wasn't the case at the old Bungalow Restaurant. Mary Haddad's French dressing was made the same in 1993, when she sold the place, as it was in the 1940s, when she and her husband, George, opened it in their home; hence the name Bungalow, after their snug little home that grew as the business did.

Put all ingredients in a jar and shake well. Cover tightly and refrigerate.

Green Goddess Dressing

Yields 1½ cups

1 (2-ounce) can anchovies

2 tablespoons wine vinegar

1 cup chopped parsley

2 tablespoons minced onion

3 tablespoons dried tarragon,
   more if fresh is used

½ cup mayonnaise

¼ cup sour cream

Parsley guarantees a lovely shade of green, and anchovies and tarragon add the flavor pizzazz. This dressing has senior status with mixed green salads. It was created in the 20s at the San Francisco Palace Hotel, in honor of George Arliss, who was appearing in a play called Green Goddess. A sauce with the same ingredients is also used for fish and shellfish.

Blend ingredients except sour cream in blender. Stir in sour cream and chill overnight.

Honey Dressing

2/3 cup sugar

1 teaspoon dry mustard

1 teaspoon paprika

1/4 teaspoon salt

1 teaspoon celery seed

1/3 cup honey

5 tablespoons vinegar

1 tablespoon lemon juice

1 teaspoon grated onion, if desired

1 cup salad oil

The bees were buzzing making honey, and Caroline and Bill Allinder were busy collecting it at their Sunnyside Bee farm, Gibsonburg, Ohio, on the sunny afternoon this recipe was jotted down. It is excellent on fruit salad or just tossed with mesclun.

Mix dry ingredients and add honey, vinegar, lemon juice, and onion, if used. Pour oil into mixture very slowly and beat constantly as it is poured.

Wine Cellar's House Mustard Dressing   Yields 1½ quarts

1 quart water

½ cup wine vinegar

2 tablespoons dry mustard

2 tablespoons Dijon mustard

2 tablespoons brown mustard

3 tablespoons sugar

2 tablespoons salt

1 tablespoon white pepper

1 tablespoon lemon juice

1 tablespoon cornstarch dissolved
    in small amount of water

1 tablespoon tarragon

2 cups vegetable oil

2 cups mayonnaise

Every salad at Toledo's long-running French Wine Cellar was served with this beautifully blended dressing made with three mustards. Chef Maximillian Korl didn't offer any alternatives.

Bring first nine ingredients to a boil and mix well during the cooking. Thicken with cornstarch; season with tarragon; and return to a slow boil. Cool.

Whisk in vegetable oil and mayonnaise.

NOTE: At the Wine Cellar, a homemade mayonnaise was used, but a good commercial product can be substituted.

Zesty Buttermilk Dressing

Yields 2 cups

1 cup low-fat yogurt

1 cup skim buttermilk

¼ cup chopped fresh parsley

2 tablespoons minced onion

½ teaspoon Mrs. Dash seasoning

¼ teaspoon dried oregano, or

    1 tablespoon fresh

¼ teaspoon dried rosemary, or

    1 tablespoon fresh

1 large garlic clove, crushed

1 tablespoon dried basil

Recommended by dietitians at the Medical College of Ohio, Toledo, this salad dressing with eight calories per tablespoon combines low-fat yogurt and skim buttermilk.

Blend yogurt and buttermilk in blender or food processor. Add other ingredients and blend. Refrigerate at least 1 hour before using.

Calories per tablespoon, 8; fat, .2 grams.

Cooked Cranberry Salad

Serves 16

1 pound fresh cranberries

2 cups water

2 cups sugar

2 envelopes unflavored gelatin

1 (20-ounce) can crushed pineapple,
    drained

¼ cup lemon juice

½ cup orange juice

1 tablespoon finely ground orange rind

1 tablespoon finely ground lemon rind

Isn't it fun to cook cranberries until they pop to signal they are done? Cooked cranberries, rather than ground fresh berries, are used in this salad with pineapple, lemon and orange juices, and rinds. The tartness of cranberry is just as welcome with grilled meats in summer as it is with the holiday turkey or ham. Buy extra berries when they are available in the fall and freeze them in the bags.

Combine cranberries, water, and sugar. Simmer, uncovered, 15 minutes. Dissolve gelatin in a little cold water. Stir quickly and thoroughly into cranberries. Stir in other ingredients. Pour into mold or bowl and refrigerate to set.

Cucumber Cheese Ring

Serves 8 to 10

1 envelope plain gelatin

1/2 cup cold water

1/2 teaspoon salt

1/2 large cucumber

3 cups small curd cottage cheese

1 (3-ounce) package cream cheese

1/2 cup salad dressing

1/2 cup onion, chopped

2/3 cup chopped celery

The refreshing flavor of cucumbers carry through cottage and cream cheeses in this attractive gelatin mold. It is one of those fill-ins when one more food which can be made a day in advance is needed for a buffet.

Soften gelatin in cold water; add salt. Put over low heat and stir until gelatin dissolves.

Pare and remove seeds from half a large cucumber; grate.

Beat cheeses with salad dressing. Stir in gelatin. Add grated cucumber, onion, and celery. Mix well before spooning into an oiled ring mold.

Chill at least 5 or 6 hours before unmolding, and, if desired, garnish plate with the other cucumber half, sliced thin.

First Prize Gelatin Plum Pudding

Serves 6

1 (3-ounce) package raspberry gelatin

1/8 teaspoon salt

1/8 teaspoon ginger

1/2 teaspoon cinnamon

1/4 teaspoon cloves

1 1/2 cups boiling water

1/2 cup raisins

1/4 cup currants

1/4 cup chopped dates

1 cup crushed pineapple, drained

1 cup chopped pecans

According to Jell-O sales, Ohioans use more of the product than residents of any other state, a statistic which prompted General Foods to sponsor a contest here. The unusual additions of spices, raisins, currants, and chopped dates to raspberry-flavored gelatin in this recipe gave Barb Doren, Swanton, Ohio, first prize. For the record, northwest Ohioans entered more recipes than other regions and won the most prizes in the contest.

Combine raspberry gelatin, salt, and spices. Dissolve in boiling water. Stir in raisins and currants. Fold in remaining ingredients. Pour into 5-cup mold and chill until firm.

Grapefruit en Gelee

Serves 8

2 pink grapefruit

¾ cup sugar

¾ cup boiling water

1½ (3-ounce) packages lemon gelatin

2 tablespoons Cointreau

Pink grapefruit only, please. The color of the fruit and its juice is the key to this tart gelatin salad which is served in the yellow grapefruit shell for a smashing presentation. It is highly recommended for brunch service as well as for lunch.

Cut grapefruit into halves. Remove seeds and fruit. Add sugar to fruit and juice and refrigerate. Clean grapefruit shells as thoroughly as possible.
Add boiling water to gelatin let stand until syrupy. Add 1 cup juice to gelatin. Add grapefruit, but no more juice. Stir in Cointreau.
Fill the 4 grapefruit shells and refrigerate to set. At serving time, cut halves into quarters and serve on greens.

Raspberry Ribbon Salad

Serves 8

Raspberry red layer:

1 envelope unflavored gelatin

1/4 cup cold water

1 (1-pound) can raspberries

1/3 cup rosé wine

Creamy cheese layer:

1 envelope unflavored gelatin

3/4 cup water

1 (3-ounce) package cream cheese

1/2 cup mayonnaise

1/2 teaspoon grated lemon peel

1 tablespoon powdered sugar

1/3 cup chopped pecans

Lime green layer:

1 (3-ounce) package lime-flavored
   gelatin

2 cups water

1/3 cup finely chopped celery

Nobody ever said layered gelatin salads are quick, but while you are waiting for each layer to set, you can start the laundry or write an overdue letter. Each of the three layers has a personality, beginning with the one featuring raspberries and rosé wine. A mold is recommended, but a 9-by-13-inch pan also can be used.

To make raspberry layer, soften gelatin in cold water. Place over hot water and heat until gelatin dissolves. Add wine and undrained raspberries; reserve a few whole raspberries for garnish. Pour into decorative 8-cup mold. Chill until almost set.

In the meantime, prepare cheese layer. Soften gelatin in cold water and dissolve over hot water. Blend cream cheese with mayonnaise, lemon peel, and powdered sugar. Add dissolved gelatin and pecans. Pour over raspberry layer. Chill until almost firm.

To prepare lime layer, dissolve gelatin in 1 cup hot water. Add 1 cup cold water. Chill until syrupy. Add celery and pour over cheese layer in mold. Chill until set.

To serve, unmold on lettuce-lined plate and garnish with dabs of mayonnaise and reserved whole raspberries.

Chicken Pasta Salad

1 pound spaghetti or vermicelli

2 cups vinaigrette

20 mushrooms, sliced

2 cups broccoli florets, blanched
    2 minutes

2 cups fresh peas, blanched,
    or frozen and defrosted

About 30 cherry tomatoes

2 cooked chicken breasts, boned,
    skinned, and cut into 1-inch cubes

2/3 cup pine nuts

2/3 cup fresh basil

Pine nuts, fresh basil and broccoli florets are the flavor treasures in this chicken pasta salad that goes main dish and first class.

Bring 5 quarts of water to a boil in large kettle. Add pasta, return to the boil and cook 4 to 7 minutes or until al dente. Drain in colander. Transfer to a large bowl; add 1 cup of the dressing. Toss and cool. Chill at least 3 hours.

Pour remaining dressing into another bowl. Add vegetables and toss to coat thoroughly.

These steps can be done in advance. When ready to serve, add chicken to the pasta; toss lightly with two forks. Add vegetables and pine nuts and chopped basil. Only fresh basil should be used in this recipe.

BASIC VINAIGRETTE: Combine 1 cup red wine vinegar, 2 teaspoons Dijon mustard, freshly ground pepper to taste in a mixing bowl and whisk briskly to blend well. Add 3 cups top quality olive oil and whisk again. This should be made 24 hours in advance. Some may want to add a whole clove of garlic and remove it when the dressing is served.

Layered Mexican Cobb Salad

Serves 6

Salad:

6 cups shredded romaine lettuce

1 (15-ounce) can red kidney beans,
    drained and rinsed

1 cup shredded Monterey Jack cheese

2 large tomatoes, diced

1½ cups diced, or shredded,
    cooked chicken

1 avocado, diced

¼ cup minced red onion

1½ cups diced jicama (or celery)

6 slices bacon, cooked and crumbled

Dressing:

⅔ cup sour cream

1 (4-ounce) can chopped green chilies,
    not drained

¼ cup chopped fresh cilantro

2 tablespoons fresh lime juice

½ teaspoon freshly ground pepper

½ teaspoon red pepper sauce

¼ teaspoon salt

Avocado, romaine, diced chicken, and crumbled bacon—the makings of a California Cobb salad—join the Mexican salad goodies of cilantro, jicama, and Monterey Jack cheese in a colorful salad bowl with a lime-cilantro dressing.

Make the dressing by combining all ingredients. Set aside.

For the salad, layer in a glass bowl the lettuce, beans, cheese, and half the tomatoes. Add chicken, avocado, onion, jicama, remaining tomatoes, and bacon in rows.

Spoon dressing over top. If desired garnish with more crumbled bacon and chopped cilantro. Toss salad with the dressing at the table.

Party Shrimp Rice Salad, Greek Style

Serves 8 to 10

4½ cups chicken broth

2 cups converted rice

⅔ cup olive oil

⅓ cup wine vinegar

½ pound cooked ham,
   cut into narrow strips

10 to 12 cherry tomatoes, halved

1 medium red or green pepper,
   cut into 1-inch strips

1 large carrot, sliced thin

1 small red onion, sliced thin and
   separated into rings

½ cup radishes, sliced thin

½ cup chopped parsley

2 tablespoons chopped fresh basil,
   or 2 teaspoons dried

2 tablespoons chopped fresh dill,
   or 1 teaspoon dried

1 pound large shrimp, cooked,
   peeled, and deveined

1 cup cubed feta cheese

1 lemon, sliced thin

Cold rice is a switch in Greek cuisine, and it happens here in grand style in a salad with confetti vegetables, crowned with feta and shrimp. Richard Nelson developed this recipe in 1984 for newspaper editors when rice salads crossed the Mason-Dixon line and moved into Ohio kitchens.

Bring chicken broth to a boil in a large saucepan. Stir in rice. Cover tightly and simmer 20 minutes. Remove from heat. Let stand covered until all liquid is absorbed, about 5 minutes. Transfer to large bowl.

Combine oil and vinegar. Add to rice, mix well. Cover and chill, stirring occasionally.

Add ham, tomatoes, peppers, carrots, onions, radishes, parsley, basil and dill to rice. Mix well. Arrange shrimp, feta cheese, and lemon slices on top of salad.

Pasta Primavera Salad

1/2 pound egg or spinach fettuccine
    noodles, or use half of each, cooked
1 bunch scallions, finely chopped
1/2 pound asparagus, blanched and
    cut on the bias (or use broccoli)
1/4 pound mushrooms, thinly sliced
1 medium zucchini, cut into
    1/2-inch rounds
2 carrots, sliced on the bias
    and blanched
1 cup pitted ripe olives
1 cup frozen peas, thawed,
    but not cooked
1 can artichoke hearts, drained
1 green pepper, diced small
1 small head cauliflower, broken into
    florets and blanched
1 pint cherry tomatoes
1/4 pound boiled ham, cut into
    julienne strips
1/4 pound summer sausage,
    cut into julienne strips
1 cup favorite Italian dressing
1/2 cup grated Parmesan cheese
Leaf lettuce

This salad is so packed with wonderful fresh foods that it's hard to find the pasta. An Italian dressing compliments the assortment of vegetables and meats.

Reserve half the cherry tomatoes and half the asparagus spears for garnish.
Combine all other vegetables and meats. Combine with pasta. Add dressing. Refrigerate 6 hours or more.
Just before serving, add Parmesan cheese, but save 3 tablespoons of it for garnish.
Spoon salad into lettuce-lined serving bowl. Garnish with cherry tomatoes, asparagus, and reserved Parmesan.

Poached Salmon Salad with Yogurt

Serves 6

6 salmon steaks, 1 inch thick

3 slices lemon

1 sprig fresh dill or 1 teaspoon dried dill

Greens

3 medium cucumbers, peeled, halved,
     seeded, and sliced thin

1 cup mayonnaise

1 cup yogurt, or sour cream

1 tablespoon chopped fresh dill

2 tablespoons chopped parsley

Garnish:

Watercress

Cherry tomatoes

Additional chopped parsley

James Beard, dean of American gastronomy, remains an idol of The Blade food editor, who had the privilege of meeting him several times. Once, when they both should have been on a diet, they shared a seat on a bus. At the end of the trip they agreed to say in unison, "1-2-3-Up" to dislodge. On another occasion he and Julia Child cooked lunch for a few editors. They burned the potatoes, but the editors ate them and loved them anyway. This salad is one of Mr. Beard's creations from 1981, when he displayed a new dependency on fresh herbs for seasoning. About the same time, he began to lower the fat in recipes, though not on himself.

Poach salmon in salted water with lemon and dill sprig. Allow 10 minutes for each inch of thickness of salmon steaks. Drain and cool. Carefully remove bone and skin; try to keep steak intact.

Arrange on a bed of greens. Combine other ingredients and spoon lavishly over each salmon steak.

Garnish with watercress and cherry tomatoes; sprinkle with more chopped parsley.

Scallops Seviche

Serves 4

½ cup dry white wine

¼ pound sea scallops

Dressing:

1 medium tomato, chopped

1 small cucumber, chopped

2 celery ribs, chopped

1 small head red leaf lettuce

1 head bibb lettuce, torn in pieces

These scallops boast a delicate white wine flavor as they join vegetables and a dressing of red wine and balsamic vinegars. Five hundred servings were made by Gladieux/Ladyfingers for The Toledo Symphony's 1994 gala benefit on the Toledo riverfront. This recipe makes four portions, which can serve as salad, fish course, or luncheon entree.

Bring white wine to a low boil. Add scallops and cook until they are no longer transparent. Drain.

Make the dressing and pour ⅓ over scallops. Chill.

Toss together tomato, cucumber, celery, red leaf lettuce and bibb lettuce; distribute onto 4 individual plates. Divide scallops among plates and dress with remaining dressing.

DRESSING: Combine 6 tablespoons virgin olive oil, 1 tablespoon red wine vinegar, 1 tablespoon balsamic vinegar, 1 tablespoon fresh lemon juice, 1 tablespoon minced fresh parsley, 1 teaspoon sugar, ½ teaspoon salt, ½ teaspoon freshly ground black pepper, and 1 minced garlic clove in jar with lid. Shake well.

Shrimp-Jicama Salad

Serves 2

1 large avocado, peeled, halved,

    and sliced thin

1 small lemon, juice and grated peel

8 ounces jicama, peeled and sliced

    into thin strips

8 large shrimp, cooked and peeled

½ bunch cilantro, trimmed,

    reserving 2 sprigs for garnish

⅔ cup yogurt

2 to 4 tablespoons salsa to taste

½ teaspoon freshly grated nutmeg

It's not certain just how cilantro and jicama slipped into heartland food culture and made such an impression. Cilantro probably rode in on a tortilla in some shape or form. Jicama slices were a mystery when they first appeared around a dip. Was it a slice of turnip, potato, or rutabaga? No, it's that new food from Mexico which just looks like a potato.

Sprinkle half of avocado slices with 1 tablespoon lemon juice. Toss with jicama strips and shrimp and divide on 2 salad plates.

Put cilantro in food processor or blender with other avocado half, 1 tablespoon lemon juice, and yogurt; blend smooth. Stir in salsa, 1 teaspoon lemon peel, and nutmeg. Spoon sauce over salads and sprinkle on a few cilantro leaves and serve.

Tuna Couscous Salad

Serves 4

1 cup uncooked couscous

1/4 cup sliced green onions

2 (6 1/2-ounce) cans solid
    white tuna in water, drained

1 (9-ounce) package frozen cut
    green beans, thawed and drained

1 (8-ounce) can sliced water
    chestnuts, drained

1/2 cup reduced-calorie mayonnaise

1/2 cup plain yogurt

2 tablespoons chopped fresh basil or
    2 teaspoons dried basil leaves

2 tablespoons cider vinegar

1/4 teaspoon salt

3 cups mixed greens cut into
    bite-sized pieces

1 large tomato, cut into 12 wedges

Couscous entered the American market place and immediately became consumer friendly. It was just what Americans were looking for. The granular semolina pasta cooks fast and is as versatile as rice. We first tasted it in the dining room at the Moroccan exhibit at Epcot Center, Walt Disney World, Florida, and couldn't wait to introduce it to northwest Ohio cooks. In Morocco, saffron is added to couscous; in Algeria it is combined with tomatoes; in Tunisia, most couscous is seasoned with hot spices; and here, we show its extreme versatility in a tuna salad with low-fat dressing.

Cook couscous as directed on package, but omit salt and margarine.

Mix couscous, onions, tuna, green beans, and water chestnuts in medium bowl.

Mix remaining ingredients, except greens and tomato wedges, and stir into couscous mixture. Cover and refrigerate about 3 hours.

Serve on greens. Garnish with tomato wedges.

Beet Salad

4 cups cooked, finely shredded beets

1 tablespoon grated horseradish

Juice of 1 lemon

½ tablespoon caraway seeds

1 cup whipping cream, beaten stiff

Canned beets work in this Eastern European inspired salad, but little compares to the earthy flavor of fresh beets.

Put cold beets in mixing bowl. Add horseradish, lemon juice, and caraway seeds. Fold in whipped cream and chill in refrigerator.
Serve on lettuce leaves.

Betty Timko's Spinach Salad

Serves 6

1 package fresh spinach

2 cups fresh, or canned, bean sprouts,
    rinsed and drained

8 slices bacon, fried crisp and crumbled

3 hard-cooked eggs, diced

Dressing (below)

In Ohio, Michigan, and Indiana supermarkets, consumers can buy Betty's Salad Dressing, which is similar to this recipe. Entrepreneur Betty Timko developed the product for the commercial market when her salad became popular in local restaurants. Mrs. Timko has been in the spotlight as a hostess, fine cook, and restaurateur since she was voted Mrs. Toledo in 1958. Occasionally the salad is made with head lettuce, but it is far better when it is made with spinach.

Make dressing and refrigerate several hours.

Clean and break spinach leaves into easy-to-eat sizes. Combine in serving bowl, with bean sprouts, bacon, and diced eggs.

Pour dressing over spinach and toss just before serving.

DRESSING: Whip together 1 cup salad oil, 3/4 cup sugar, 1/3 cup ketchup, 1/4 cup vinegar, 1 tablespoon Worcestershire sauce, 1 medium onion (grated), and salt. The dressing will keep 2 to 3 weeks in a covered container in the refrigerator.

photo on cover

Black Bean and Yellow Rice Salad

Serves 4

2 cups water

1 cup uncooked rice

1/2 teaspoon powdered turmeric

1 teaspoon vegetable oil

1 teaspoon salt

2 1/2 cups cooked black beans

1 cup diced tomato

1/2 cup diced roasted red peppers

1/4 cup chopped onion

2 tablespoons lemon juice

2 tablespoons olive oil

1 tablespoon white vinegar

Hot sauce, to taste

1 avocado, diced

Black beans and yellow rice make a smashing presentation that is as healthful as it is attractive. Avocado and tomato add further color and flavor interest. Beans, once considered peasant food, have moved into gourmet status in the 90s because they are a high-fiber, low-fat source of protein. Nutritionists don't talk much about price, but beans are as low in price as they are high in nutrients.

In medium saucepan, heat water to boiling. Add rice, turmeric, oil, and salt. Cover, lower heat, and cook until rice is tender, about 20 minutes. Cool slightly.

Combine beans, tomato, red peppers, onion, lemon juice, olive oil, vinegar, and hot sauce. Gently toss with rice. Garnish with avocado.

Cauliflower with Spinach Dressing

1 small head cauliflower, uncooked

1 onion, thinly sliced

1 (3½-ounce) bottle stuffed green olives, sliced

¼ cup Roquefort cheese (or bleu cheese)

1 small head lettuce

1 avocado, sliced

1 can artichoke hearts, drained

½ cup Spinach Dressing

Cheddar cheese croutons

Here is one way to pack many goodies into one salad. It is loaded with such treasures as avocado and artichoke hearts and a spinach dressing that's really green. Keep the dressing recipe handy to use with other fresh vegetable salads.

Break cauliflower into small pieces; add sliced onions, olives, and crumbled bleu cheese. Gently stir avocado and artichoke hearts. Break lettuce into small pieces.

Toss together, pour spinach dressing over all. Add croutons and toss lightly again.

SPINACH DRESSING: Combine 6 tablespoons salad oil, juice of ½ lemon, 1 tablespoon chopped parsley, ½ cup finely chopped fresh spinach, and 1 small onion, finely chopped, in a glass jar and shake vigorously.

photo page 142

Chef Louis' Spring Salad

Serves 8

½ pound fresh asparagus
1 bunch watercress
8 ounces fresh spinach
4 ounces fresh snow peas, trimmed
4 to 6 pencil-thin spring carrots, about 5 inches long

Dressing:

½ cup each: salad oil and either rice vinegar or balsamic vinegar
¼ cup water
½ cup each: watercress stems and spinach stems, chopped
Reserve chopped asparagus from above
1 small bunch fresh tarragon or fresh basil, or a mixture of any two or three of the following: flat-leaf parsley, tarragon, basil, chives, or green onion tops, chopped, to make 2 to 3 tablespoons
2 tablespoons Worcestershire sauce
1 cup mayonnaise
½ teaspoon salt
½ teaspoon sugar
¼ teaspoon freshly ground black pepper

Chef Louis Szmathary's salad bursts with all things fresh, from asparagus to tarragon. The Hungarian-born chef, who gained national fame at The Bakery in Chicago, was a favorite as the celebrity chef at The Blade-sponsored food fairs.

Wash, shake, dry, and chill all salad ingredients. Peel asparagus and cut at sharp angle into ¼-inch thick ovals. Chop bottom ½-inch of stalks to add to dressing. Snip ends from snow peas and use whole and cut some into pieces. Reserve carrots.

Add all dressing ingredients to blender except mayonnaise, salt, sugar, and pepper. Blend at high speed to a frothy green liquid with flecks of green in it. In a bowl, gently fold in mayonnaise, salt, sugar, and pepper. Taste and correct seasoning.

Arrange salad ingredients on individual plates and spoon on dressing generously. Pare and grate carrots coarsely and sprinkle over top.

Cold Asparagus Vinaigrette

Serves 4

2 pounds asparagus, trimmed and, if
desired, peeled (only large stalks
require peeling)

1 small shallot, minced

1 small garlic clove, crushed

1/2 teaspoon salt

1 1/2 teaspoons Dijon mustard

Juice of 1/2 lemon

3/4 cup vegetable or olive oil

2 teaspoons red wine vinegar

1/2 teaspoon freshly ground black pepper

1 hard-cooked egg, yolk and
white minced separately

1/4 cup chopped fresh parsley

In early spring people walk along the roadside with paper bags in one hand, a knife in the other, and their noses to the ground. They are asparagus hunters. The season for the local slender green stalks with an incomparable fresh taste is all too short, and it seems we can't get enough. That explains two pounds of asparagus for four servings in this salad with a Dijon mustard vinaigrette. Or should it be just two servings?

Cook asparagus until barely done and drain well. Arrange spears in shallow serving dish and sprinkle with minced shallot. Place garlic and salt in small bowl; mash to a paste with back of a spoon. Stir in mustard and lemon juice. Whisk in oil, vinegar, and pepper. Spoon over asparagus.

Garnish with alternating bands of chopped egg white, parsley, and egg yolk. Chill thoroughly before serving.

Down on the Muck Spinach Salad

Serves 6

1 package fresh spinach, chopped

3 to 4 slices cooked bacon, crumbled

3 to 4 hard-cooked egg, chopped

Dressing(below)

As fresh as the green fields in Celeryville, Ohio, a spinach salad with bacon and onion is dressed with vinegar and oil. Celeryville is 3,000 acres of black muck in north central Ohio, where celery and salad greens paint a beautiful picture.

Combine chopped spinach with crumbled bacon and chopped egg. Add dressing to salad just before serving.

DRESSING: Combine the following ingredients a few hours before serving to allow the flavors to develop: 1/4 cup vinegar, 1/2 cup sugar, 1/2 cup vegetable oil, chopped onion to taste, salt, and pepper.

Jicama Watercress Salad

Serves 4 to 6

1 medium jicama, about 1 pound

3 to 4 radishes

1 orange

2 small bunches watercress, cleaned and
    stems removed

2 tablespoons fresh cilantro, chopped

Romaine lettuce for garnish

Herb dressing (below)

This salad with a delightful chive blossom vinegar and olive oil herb dressing is credited to Georgeann Brown, Dundee, Michigan. Her trendy salad is in stark contrast to her hobby of hearth cooking with antique tools in a specially designed fireplace in the Brown home.

Make dressing and set aside. Peel jicama and cut into pieces the size of matchsticks. Thinly slice radishes and combine with jicama in large mixing bowl.

Peel orange with knife and cut away all white pith and exterior membrane. Remove orange slices and cut into smaller pieces and add to the bowl. Add watercress, cilantro, and dressing to jicama mixture. Let stand several minutes. Toss occasionally.

Line large serving plate with romaine leaves. Mound salad onto center of leaves.

HERB DRESSING: Process zest of 1 orange, ½ cup chive blossom vinegar (or use cider vinegar), 1 cup olive oil, 1 teaspoon ground allspice berries, ¼ teaspoon ground black peppercorns, ¼ teaspoon whole thyme leaves, and 1 teaspoon salt until thoroughly combined and orange zest is chopped fine.

Lentil Confetti Salad

Yields 1¾ quarts

1/2 pound lentils

3 cups water

1½ teaspoons salt

2 cups cooked rice

1 cup Italian dressing

1 cup diced tomatoes

1/2 cup chopped green peppers

1/2 cup chopped onion

1/4 cup each: chopped celery, chopped
     pimiento, sliced green olives

Requests from Bowling Green State University students for more vegetarian selections in the cafeteria brought responses such as this salad from the food service management team. Italian dressing brightens the rice; lentils, tomatoes, and green peppers keep it in the vegetarian classification.

Rinse lentils under cold water and drain. Bring water, lentils, and salt to a boil. Reduce heat. Simmer, covered, about 20 minutes or until just tender. Drain immediately.

Combine lentil mixture with cooked rice. Pour dressing over and refrigerate until cold. Before serving, stir in remaining ingredients and mix well.

Orange Pico Salad

4 oranges, peeled, sliced, seeded, drained,

    and the juice saved

1 cucumber, not pared but sliced thin

6 cups torn spinach leaves,

    about 1½ pounds

2 heads bibb lettuce, torn

1 small red onion, sliced and

    separated into rings

½ cup coarsely chopped,

    toasted walnuts

Orange vinaigrette dressing

It is important to follow the directions for the assembly of this attractive salad, outlined with cucumber and orange cartwheels. Red onion rings and toasted walnuts join greens in the center, and an orange vinaigrette add the finishing touch.

Arrange several orange and cucumber slices alternately around sides of chilled, large, glass salad bowl. Arrange spinach, bibb lettuce, and remaining orange and cucumber slices, onion rings, and walnuts in layers in bowl.

ORANGE VINAIGRETTE DRESSING: Place in jar ½ cup vegetable oil, 2 tablespoons cider vinegar, ¼ teaspoon salt, ¼ cup reserved orange juice, 1½ teaspoons sugar, and ⅛ teaspoon freshly ground pepper. Cover jar and shake to mix. Pour over salad just before it is served.

Sherbrooke's Caesar Salad

Serves 8-10

2 garlic cloves

4 tablespoons olive oil

6 anchovies, cut into small pieces

3 heads romaine, washed, dried,
   and broken into fair size pieces
   and chilled

Juice of 2 lemons

4 (1-minute) coddled eggs

1 teaspoon freshly ground
   black pepper

1/2 teaspoon white pepper,
   freshly ground

1 teaspoon dry mustard

2 teaspoons Worcestershire sauce

3 drops hot pepper sauce

1 cup half-inch croutons

In a 1964 column, it was reported, "Bill Zouhary is the perfect restaurateur to feature Caesar Salad, for it demands a gracious host who enjoys patrons enough to spend the time at the table mixing the salad's ingredients and tossing and serving it with great gusto. The person must have a deep feeling about food, for in every step there is love as well as lemon, garlic, anchovies and eggs." With such praise, Mr. Zouhary decided to release the secret recipe for publication. His first rule: "Don't cut the romaine, break it."

At least 24 hours before the salad is to be made, finely chop garlic cloves and add them to the olive oil in a container from which they can be poured. Chop anchovies fine before the salad is made.

Place prepared greens in large wooden bowl.

In a smaller bowl, mash anchovies into a paste. Add garlic and olive oil mixture and lemon juice and continue to mash into a smooth blend. Add eggs, 1 at a time, and mix into the dressing. Add both peppers, mustard, Worcestershire sauce, and hot pepper sauce. Mix dressing well. Pour over greens, add croutons, and cheese. Toss and serve immediately.

Shredded Carrots with Cumin and Pine Nuts

Serves 6

4 cups coarsely shredded carrots

2 tablespoons chopped cilantro

2 tablespoons pine nuts, toasted
   in warm skillet

1½ teaspoons ground cumin;
   more, if desired

2 tablespoons fresh lime juice

2 teaspoons seeded and finely
   chopped jalapeño peppers

3 tablespoons olive oil

½ teaspoon salt, or to taste

Carrots, the versatile standby that is added to everything from roast beef to relish trays, take to the hot, spicy 90s with cumin and jalapeños in this tantalizing salad. Pine nuts, cilantro, and lime juice add to the uniqueness and good flavor. The food editor dares you to take it to the family reunion or church supper.

Combine carrots and cilantro in medium bowl. Heat and stir pine nuts in skillet over low heat until golden, about 2 minutes. Pour into dish.

Add cumin to skillet and heat over very low heat until warm and fragrant, about 1 minute. Stir in lime juice, chopped jalapeño, olive oil, and salt.

Pour dressing over carrot and cilantro mixture. Toss well. Sprinkle with pine nuts.

Toledo Tabbouleh

Serves 6

1½ cups cracked wheat (bulgar)

5 bunches parsley

½ cup fresh mint, or 1 tablespoon
   dried mint

7 medium tomatoes

Juice of 5 lemons

1 cup olive oil

Salt and pepper

Dash cinnamon

1 bunch green onions

No one leaves the parsley on the plate when eating this salad. It is loaded with the fresh-flavored herb which is high in vitamins A and C. The recipe is from the Ansara family of chefs, who cooked in Toledo restaurants for many years. The Ansaras always managed to feature their native Lebanese foods in their all-American steak houses.

Wash and soak cracked wheat in water 10 minutes. Clean, wash, and chop vegetables fine. Squeeze water from wheat and combine with vegetables. Combine with lemon juice, oil, salt, pepper, and cinnamon. Refrigerate.

If desired, garnish with feta cheese and olives. Serve with lettuce leaves or pita triangles.

Waldorf Salad with Homemade Dressing

Serves 8

6 to 7 apples, unpared, cubed

2 cups whole grapes

1 cup miniature marshmallows

1 cup chopped walnuts

1½ cups chopped celery

2 cans pineapple chunks, well-drained,

    but juice reserved (about 1½ cups)

Dressing:

1½ cups reserved pineapple juice

2 tablespoons flour

3 eggs, beaten

¾ to 1 cup sugar

Midwesterners long ago adopted the Waldorf Hotel's apple salad as their very own. This version is from the Patchwork Quilt, Middlebury, Indiana, in Amish country, where home cooking is a way of life.

To make dressing: Combine pineapple juice and flour in top of double boiler. Blend in beaten eggs and stir in sugar. Cook and stir and bring to a boil. Cool before adding to salad mixture.

Combine all Waldorf salad ingredients and mix with dressing.

Breads & Sandwiches

Breads cover a wide range of specialty foods. They are not just the fragrant loaves of yeast breads that someone watched over for hours or the high-rise healthful bran muffins that are baked morning fresh and slathered with butter and jam.

Breads include pancakes hot off the griddle made from Elmer Madden's recipe, homemade noodles, and matzo balls which float in chicken broth.

The staff of life circles the globe in many styles and returns home with southern-style Boone Tavern Spoon Bread and biscuits for shortcake. Deep-fried Indian Poori compliments curries. Swedish Limpa is fragrant with molasses and caraway. Breads pick up fascinating textures with the introduction of herbs and seeds.

The English Earl of Sandwich gets credit for putting a filling between two slices of bread. Then the Americans introduced an incredible mix of breads, fillings, and spreads, becoming world champion sandwich makers.

Whatever the current trend, we find a way to adapt it into a sandwich. The Open-Faced Pizza Submarine gathers popular pizza ingredients on French bread. Grace Smith's Open-Faced Sandwich, which dates from the 1950s, has a new audience of people with vegetarian dietary habits.

On opposite page: The goodness of grains is featured in pancakes, corn muffins, and cornbread. Photographed at the Ludwig Mill, an historic landmark at Grand Rapids, Ohio.

Pennsylvania Dutch Funnel Cakes

Serves 8

3 eggs

2 cups milk

4 cups flour

1/2 teaspoon salt

2 teaspoons baking powder

2 tablespoons sugar

Vegetable oil

Funnel cakes are a slice of Americana which have been revived at fairs and festivals, where people stand in line and patiently wait for the deep-fried, coiled cakes dusted with powdered sugar. It is said that Pennsylvania farmers returned to the house after morning chores for a funnel cake and a cup of coffee. They are named funnel, because that is the best tool with which to make them. Batter is poured through a funnel, around and around, in a circular motion into hot grease. A pitcher with a narrow lip works, too.

Beat eggs and add other ingredients to make a waffle-like batter. Heat 2 inches of vegetable oil in an iron skillet to 350 degrees (very hot). Pour the batter through a funnel in a coil-like pattern into the grease, and fry until brown.

Serve sprinkled with powdered sugar or with molasses or syrup.

NOTE: It is important that an iron skillet be used, and that the shortening be deep and hot enough.

Indian Poori

2 cups whole-wheat flour

1/2 cup unbleached flour

1/2 teaspoon salt

3 teaspoons oil

Water

Additional oil for frying

"Come on over and I'll teach you to cook Indian foods," Ranjana Bhasin offered. Soon the invitation spread around town, and Mrs. Bhasin had a full schedule of cooking classes in the kitchen of her home. Among the foods prepared was poori, the puffed, deep-fried, Indian bread that is the perfect accompaniment to curries and dal.

Combine flours and salt. Add oil and enough water to make a stiff dough. Knead for at least 10 minutes and let rest 1/2 hour. Knead again.

Pinch off small balls of dough. Flatten and roll out into circles about 4 inches across.

Heat vegetable oil to smoking hot and drop 1 disk of dough at a time into it. When the dough hits the hot grease push it down with a spatula, then let it puff up; turn it over to cook on the other side. If the circle of dough is cut even slightly it will not puff. Drain on paper towels.

Refrigerator Bran Muffins

Yields 90 to 100 muffins

2 cups boiling water

6 cups 100% bran cereal, divided

3 cups sugar

1 cup vegetable shortening

4 beaten eggs

5 cups flour

5 teaspoons soda

1½ teaspoons salt

1 quart buttermilk

This is one of those recipes a food writer feels committed to include in a cookbook to avoid having someone say, "Wonder how she forgot the bran muffin recipe." It's a golden oldie that is as good as it was when it made the rounds in the 70s. The batter keeps, refrigerated, for six weeks. Just dip into it and bake a few at a time.

Pour boiling water over 2 cups of bran cereal. Set aside. Cream shortening with sugar. Add eggs; beat until combined. Stir in flour, soda, and salt. Mix well.

Add remaining 4 cups bran cereal and buttermilk; mix. Bake in greased muffin tins 15 to 20 minutes in 400-degree oven, or refrigerate and bake as needed.

Pumpkin Apple Streusel Muffins

Yields 22 muffins

2 1/2 cups flour

1 1/2 cups sugar

1 tablespoon pumpkin pie spice

1 teaspoon soda

1/2 teaspoon salt

1/2 cup oil

1 cup canned pumpkin

2 eggs

2 cups peeled, finely chopped apples

Streusel topping:

2 tablespoons flour

4 tablespoons sugar

1/2 teaspoon cinnamon

4 teaspoons butter

Beyond pies, Ohioans find many ways to bake with home-grown apples. Here they are again, starring in muffins with a buttery streusel top. Several readers sent in this recipe, saying it was especially good. Finally, the food editor tried it and had to agree.

Sift flour, sugar, pumpkin pie spice, soda, and salt in a mixing bowl. Add the oil, pumpkin, and eggs, one at a time, mixing after each addition. Gently stir in apples. Spoon batter into greased or paper-lined muffin cups, filling 3/4 full.

Make topping by combining flour, sugar, and cinnamon. Cut in butter. Sprinkle topping over batter. Bake at 350 degrees for 35 to 40 minutes.

Southern-Style Biscuits

Yields 12 biscuits

2 1/2 cups flour

1 teaspoon sugar

1/2 teaspoon baking soda

1 1/2 teaspoons baking powder

1 teaspoon salt

1/2 cup soft shortening

2/3 cup buttermilk, or a little more

Every new cook, and perhaps a lot of experienced cooks, too, should learn to make biscuits. It takes a little practice, but even the mistakes taste pretty good. Biscuits serve several purposes. As an example, these old-fashioned buttermilk biscuits that are baked in a round cake pan have a split personality. When sugar is added to the batter, they are destined for fruit and berry shortcakes, but when the sugar is eliminated, they bake atop stews or are a base for hot chicken or tuna à la king. Hot biscuits for breakfast with honey is another way such homespun goodness is enjoyed.

Sift flour, sugar, baking soda, baking powder, and salt. Blend in shortening with fork or pastry blender. Add buttermilk as dough is kneaded, to make a soft ball. Knead briefly. Roll out on lightly floured surface to at least 1/2 inch thick and cut with biscuit cutter.

Grease 9-inch round cake pan. Fit biscuits into pan tightly together. Bake in 450-degree oven 12 to 15 minutes until lightly browned.

The sugar can be eliminated for stew toppings and other uses. It is added for shortcake biscuits to brown them.

Banana Oatmeal Bread

Yields 1 loaf

1/2 cup shortening

1 cup sugar

2 eggs

1/2 teaspoon vanilla

1 cup flour

1 cup quick oatmeal

1 teaspoon baking soda

1/2 teaspoon salt

1/2 teaspoon cinnamon

1 1/2 cups mashed bananas,
    about 3 medium

1/4 cup milk

1/2 cup chopped raisins

This is the best banana bread we have ever baked, and goodness knows in 41 years a lot of over-ripe bananas have been destined for a batch of quick bread. This one is favored because it is made with oatmeal, which keeps it moist. Each time the subject turns to bananas, we recall the day we took six banana baked goods to the ape house at the Toledo Zoo. Along with cookies, bread, cakes, etc., we took a table, lace cloth, and candelabrum to add to the photo setup. When everything was in place, and the monkeys stared down at the table in disbelief, the photographer said, "Are you going to get any more crazy ideas?" That was in January. The next summer we took cold soups to be photographed with the polar bears at the zoo. Fortunately, it was a different photographer, which may have saved the food editor's life.

Cream shortening and sugar. Add eggs and vanilla and beat until fluffy. Combine dry ingredients and add to first mixture alternately with bananas and milk. Mix well and fold in raisins.

Bake in greased 9-by-5-inch loaf pan 50 to 60 minutes in 350-degree oven. Cover for 5 minutes after being removed from oven to keep the moisture in the bread.

Boone Tavern Spoon Bread

Yields 2 casseroles

3 cups milk

1¼ cups white cornmeal

3 eggs

1¾ teaspoons baking powder

1 teaspoon salt

2 tablespoons butter, melted

One reason to have lunch or dinner at the Boone Tavern at Berea, Kentucky, is this traditional southern bread that, like the name indicates, is spooned and not sliced. The dining room and hotel are operated by Berea College students who are hospitable in the southern manner.

Stir cornmeal into rapidly boiling milk. Cook until thick, stirring constantly. Remove from heat; cool.

When mixture is cold and stiff, add beaten eggs, salt, baking powder, and melted butter. Beat 15 minutes; then beat another 10 minutes with a wooden spoon.

Pour into two well-greased casseroles. Bake 30 minutes in 375-degree oven. Serve with spoon.

Canyon Ranch Bread

Yields 1 loaf, 18 slices

1½ cups whole wheat flour

1 cup unprocessed wheat bran

1 tablespoon baking powder

¼ teaspoon baking soda

3 tablespoons fructose

1 teaspoon ground cinnamon

⅓ cup raisins, finely chopped

1⅓ cups buttermilk

1 egg, lightly beaten

4 teaspoons vanilla extract

Straight from the fitness center at Canyon Ranch, Tucson, Arizona, this is a country whole wheat buttermilk bread with only 60 calories a slice.

Mix flour, wheat bran, baking powder, soda, fructose, and cinnamon in large bowl. Add raisins; mix well. Combine buttermilk, egg, and vanilla in another bowl; mix well.

Pour liquid ingredients into dry ingredients, mixing well. Pour mixture into a standard size non-stick bread pan.

Bake 50 minutes in a 350-degree oven. Place the bread on its side on a wire rack to cool.

Honey Pecan-Date Bread

Yields 1 loaf

1½ cups whole wheat flour

1¼ cups all-purpose flour

1 teaspoon salt

½ teaspoon baking soda

2 teaspoons baking powder

1 egg

1 cup milk

¾ cup honey

2 tablespoons butter, melted
     and cooled

½ cup chopped dates

½ cup chopped pecans dusted
     with flour

Everyone claims to be counting calories and fat grams. Still, there is rarely a meeting, whether it is a small committee or a large organization, where some food is not served. This is a committee meeting sort of bread; one which can be made in advance, refrigerated, and then sliced thin and served with cream cheese. A little orange juice beaten into the cream cheese takes it one easy step further.

Sift dry ingredients. Set aside. Beat egg until light. Add milk, honey, and melted butter. Slowly add dry ingredients to liquid. Continue to blend until well mixed. Fold in chopped dates and pecans.

Turn dough into well-greased and floured loaf pan. Bake 1 hour at 350-degrees.

Pumpkin-Cranberry Nut Bread

Yields 2 loaves

3½ cups flour

2 teaspoons ground cinnamon

1 teaspoon salt

1 teaspoon baking soda

½ teaspoon baking powder

2 teaspoons grated orange rind

¾ cup butter, softened

2 cups sugar

3 eggs

1 (1-pound) can pumpkin

1 cup chopped walnuts

1 cup chopped cranberries

Our favorite holiday bread, bar none. Pumpkin keeps it moist. Cranberries give it color and texture. Orange peel is also an important contributor. This is a bread that can be proudly given as a gift.

Combine dry ingredients, including orange rind, and set aside. Cream butter and sugar. Add eggs, 1 at a time, and mix well after each addition. Alternate additions of pumpkin and dry ingredients. Stir in nuts and cranberries. Pour batter into 2 lightly greased 8½-inch-by 4½-by-2½-inch loaf pans. Bake 1 hour, or a little longer, until it tests done in the center.

If desired, drizzle with icing made by mixing just enough milk or cream into confectioners' sugar to make a slightly runny consistency. For the holidays, decorate with walnut halves. Wrap well. It freezes well.

Tex-Mex Corn Bread

Yields 1 large loaf

2 cups yellow cornmeal

6 teaspoons baking powder

2 cups shredded Cheddar cheese

4 eggs

1 cup vegetable oil

1 cup sour cream

2 tablespoons diced pimiento

1 (1-pound) can cream-style corn

2 (4-ounce) cans green chilies, diced

Really, now, corn bread baked in a bundt pan? Yes, and this is a show stopper. It's bright with pimiento and green chilies and extended with canned corn and cheese. Best of all, it's just the ticket to accompany chili.

Grease and lightly flour bundt pan. Combine cornmeal, baking powder, and cheese in large bowl. In a medium bowl, whisk eggs, oil, and sour cream. Stir in pimiento, corn, and chilies until they are well-combined. Add to cornmeal mixture and stir just until moistened.

Spoon into prepared pan. Bake 1 hour in 400-degree oven. Remove from oven and let stand on wire rack 10 minutes before removing from pan, but try to serve piping hot. The recipe can be reduced by half.

Elmer's Buttermilk Pancakes

Yields 1 gallon batter

1 quart cold water

1 quart buttermilk

4 eggs

1 pint corn oil

1 cup sugar

1 heaping tablespoon baking soda

2 tablespoons salt

2 tablespoons vanilla

3½ pounds all-purpose flour

2 heaping tablespoons baking powder

Elmer Madden was the fastest grill cook in the Midwest. From early morning until after lunch, he stood guard at the grill of his little corner cafe and cooked each egg, hamburger, or sausage patty with loving care. Breakfast customers still remember the pile of sliced potatoes ready for hearty eaters and the beautiful tender buttermilk pancakes that nearly covered a dinner plate. When he was asked for the recipe, Mr. Madden admitted he just never followed one, but together he and the food editor figured it out.

Put ingredients into bowl in the order given and beat for 20 minutes. The batter will keep up to 3 weeks, covered in the refrigerator.

There are about 4 cups of flour per pound.

Puffy German Pancake

Serves 4

2 tablespoons butter

4 eggs

2/3 cup flour

1 tablespoon sugar

1/2 teaspoon salt

2/3 cup milk

Have the powdered sugar and lemon juice on the table. When this big puffed pancake comes out of the oven, it should be served immediately. There's no time to look for the sugar, or even to squeeze the lemon. This is a weekend breakfast delight.

Preheat oven to 400 degrees. Put butter into a 16-inch heavy, ovenproof skillet and place in oven until butter melts and skillet is very hot.

Combine other ingredients and beat at least 2 minutes until smooth. Pour immediately into hot skillet and place in 400-degree oven. Bake 20 to 25 minutes until batter has climbed up the sides of the skillet, and edges are brown and puffy.

Cut immediately into wedges to be served with butter, powdered sugar, and lemon juice. Alternate toppings are sautéed apples, crumbled bacon, or fresh fruit.

Cornish Pasties

Filling:

1 pound sirloin steak, cut into
   1/4-inch cubes

3 or 4 medium potatoes, pared and
   chopped fine

5 green onions, minced, including the
   green tops

Salt and pepper to taste

Finely chopped, pared rutabagas and
   carrots (optional)

Pastry crust:

1 cup shortening

1 tablespoon butter

4 cups flour

1 teaspoon salt

1/2 teaspoon baking powder

About 6 tablespoons ice water

1 egg, slightly beaten

1 tablespoon milk

Meat and vegetable filled pastry turnovers, these pasties originated in Cornwall, England, as a lunch for copper miners. They are shaped to be tucked into a pocket. Copper mining families brought the custom from England to the Upper Peninsula of Michigan when mines opened there. Rutabagas make the filling authentic, but even though lard was used for the pastry in the original recipe, it has been updated with vegetable shortening.

Combine meat and vegetables in a large bowl and season to taste. Mix well. To make the pastry, cut shortening and butter into flour that has been well mixed with salt and baking powder. Add enough ice water to make a stiff dough.

Divide the dough into 2 parts and roll out on lightly floured board to 1/4-inch thickness. Cut dough into 5-inch circles or, if desired, larger circles.

Place a small portion of the meat and vegetables in the center of each circle. Moisten the edges with water to insure sealing. Fold pastry over filling and seal and crimp tightly.

Beat egg and milk and brush over pasties. Make a small hole in each one to allow the steam to escape. Bake 1 hour on cookie sheet in 375-degree oven. If they become too brown during that time, cover with foil.

Grace Smith's Vegetable Sandwich

Yields 15

Cheese Spread:

1½ cups shredded Cheddar cheese

1 cup shredded soft American cheese

1 teaspoon dry mustard

1 teaspoon Worcestershire sauce

1 teaspoon paprika

⅓ cup mayonnaise

Sandwiches:

4 pounds shredded cabbage

2 pounds shredded carrots

2 cups diced green peppers

1 teaspoon hot pepper sauce

1 teaspoon salt

2 cups mayonnaise

Tomato slices

Toast

This open-faced vegetable sandwich tells a lot about its creator, Grace Smith, who started her career in 1910 when she took over the YWCA cafeteria in downtown Toledo. She then operated her own large cafeteria for many years. She gained national fame and was the only woman president of the National Restaurant Association. Miss Smith had a penchant for fresh ingredients. Back in the 50s, the array of vegetables and salads in the cafeteria offered customers a rainbow of healthful eating. In the 90s her sandwich is making a grand re-entry.

Combine shredded Cheddar and shredded American cheese at room temperature, with dry mustard, Worcestershire sauce, paprika, and ⅓ cup mayonnaise. Set spread aside.

Combine cabbage, carrots, green pepper, hot pepper sauce, salt, and 2 cups mayonnaise. Arrange tomato slices on toast, spread vegetable mixture evenly over it, and top with cheese spread. Place under broiler to brown.

Greek-Style Gyros

Serves 2

1/4 cup yogurt

2 tablespoons diced cucumber

1 1/2 teaspoons olive oil

8 ounces breakfast beef steaks,
    cut 1/4-inch thick

4 thin onion slices, separated into rings

1 garlic clove, minced

1/2 teaspoon dried oregano leaves

1/4 teaspoon salt

Dash pepper

6 tomato slices

1 pita bread, cut in half and warmed

Yogurt, fresh vegetables, and limited meat puts the centuries-old style of Greek sandwich in the healthful league. The neatly packaged sandwich is dependent on pita pocket bread. You can mix and match the fillings, but this is a start in the right direction.

Combine yogurt, cucumber, and 1/2 teaspoon oil. Cut beef into 1/2-inch wide strips. Cut each strip in half. Cook and stir onion, garlic, and oregano in remaining oil in non-stick frying pan over medium high heat for 1 minute.

Add and stir-fry beef 1 to 1 1/2 minutes, or until lightly browned. Do not overcook. Season with salt and pepper.

Place 3 tomato slices and an equal amount of meat mixture into each pita half. Serve with cucumber-yogurt sauce.

Open-Faced Pizza Submarine

Serves 10 to 12

2 loaves French bread

2 pounds ground beef

2 cups tomato paste

1 cup chopped ripe olives

1 cup Parmesan cheese

1 teaspoon oregano

1 teaspoon basil

2 teaspoons salt

Pepper to taste

Mozzarella cheese slices

A loaf of French bread splits to make two thick bases for a savory ground beef mixture topped with mozzarella cheese slices.

Cut French bread into halves, lengthwise. Mix all ingredients except cheese slices and spread fairly thickly on bread halves, being sure to spread to the edges. Arrange cheese slices on top.

Wrap and refrigerate at least an hour, but longer won't hurt.

Bake, uncovered, on cookie sheets, in 350-degree oven for 30 minutes. To serve, cut into wide chunks.

Pepperoni Loaf

1 (16-ounce) loaf frozen bread dough

2 (3½ ounce) packages sliced pepperoni

6 to 8 ounces sliced provolone cheese

Cornmeal

Easy does it with three ingredients pulled from the freezer and refrigerator. These filled dough circles are open-faced, main dish sandwiches.

Thaw frozen bread dough according to package directions. On lightly floured surface, roll thawed dough into a 9-by-12-inch rectangle.

Layer pepperoni and cheese slices over dough to within ½ inch of the edges. Roll up jelly-roll style, starting with long side. Seal edges and ends.

Place sealed side down on greased baking sheet that has been sprinkled with cornmeal. Bake 40 minutes in 350-degree oven until golden. Cool slightly before slicing.

Belly Stickers

1 package yeast

1/2 cup water

1/2 cup sugar, plus 1 teaspoon

1 1/2 cups milk

1/2 cup solid shortening

2 teaspoons salt

2 eggs, beaten

7 to 7 1/2 cups flour

Topping:

1/2 cup sugar

1/3 cup half and half

1 teaspoon vanilla sugar

Archbold, Ohio, in a fertile farming district, claims these unique upside-down yeast rolls that hark to the days when fresh cream from the barn was just a reach away. Farm women still make them, and they are sold at the Doughbox at Sauder's Farm Museum Village, near Archbold. The recipe is from Donna Gnagey, who has operated the Doughbox for 20 years. Just before the rolls are baked, heavy cream is poured over and sugar is sprinkled over the top. The sugar and cream slide to the bottom of the baking pan. When the baked rolls are turned over, the cream and sugar becomes the topping, and—they say—sticks to the belly. Exactly what is needed after morning chores.

Dissolve yeast and 1 teaspoon sugar in 1/2 cup warm water. Scald milk and shortening together. Cool to lukewarm. Add 1/2 cup sugar, salt, beaten eggs, and yeast mixture. Add flour gradually, mixing first with a spoon, then by hand. Knead 5 minutes on floured board.

Cover and let dough rise to double in size. Roll into balls the size of walnuts. Fit 18 dough balls in a buttered 10 inch pie pan. Cover and let rise to double in size. Before placing in the oven, make topping. Combine sugar, half and half, and vanilla. Pour over rolls. It will go to the bottom of the pan.

Bake in 375-degree oven, about 25 to 30 minutes, until golden brown. Use remaining dough for more belly stickers or as sweet rolls.

Photo on cover

Pluckets

1 cup scalded milk

1/3 cup sugar

1/2 cup shortening

1/2 teaspoon salt

1 package yeast, dissolved in

    1/4 cup warm water

3 eggs, well beaten

5 cups flour

Melted butter

1 cup more sugar

3 teaspoons cinnamon

1/3 cup finely chopped nuts

Dough balls stacked in a tube pan bake together to form an irresistible pyramid of buttery, nut-coated breakfast rolls. As the name instructs, they are plucked off one by one.

Add sugar, shortening, and salt to scalded milk. When lukewarm, add mixture to dissolved yeast and eggs; gradually add to flour. Beat thoroughly. Cover and let rise until doubled. It is a very soft dough. Stir down and let rise again until doubled. Stir together sugar, cinnamon, and nuts. Take a rounded teaspoon of dough and dip into melted butter; roll in sugar-cinnamon-nuts mixture. Pile pieces loosely in ungreased tube pan. There should be enough for 2 layers. Let rise 30 minutes, or longer. Bake 30 minutes in 350-degree oven, or until done.

When baked, turn upside down immediately. The rolls will be stuck together and are served that way, letting everyone pluck off one or two. They can be reheated in the oven if wrapped in foil.

Sticky Buns

Yields 12 servings

1/2 cup chopped pecans

2 loaves frozen bread dough, thawed

2 (3-ounce) packages regular vanilla

    pudding (not instant)

1 cup brown sugar

1/2 cup butter

2 tablespoons milk

1 1/2 teaspoons cinnamon

Out of yeast? Little time to bake? Frozen dough comes to the rescue and packaged pudding mix gives a helping hand here in hot-from-the-oven pecan rolls with a homemade look.

Heavily butter 9-by-13-inch baking pan. Sprinkle pecans over bottom of pan. Tear one loaf of thawed bread into small pieces and place over bottom of pan on pecans.

Combine pudding, brown sugar, butter, milk, and cinnamon in saucepan. Bring to a boil and pour over bread pieces.

Break up second loaf of thawed bread into pieces and arrange on sauce over first layer. Cover and let rise 1 1/2 to 2 hours.

Bake about 30 minutes in 350-degree oven. Flip pan to serve with the pecans on top.

Sunday Morning Nut Rolls

Yields 18 rolls

1 package yeast

1 cup lukewarm sweet cream

1 cup butter

5 egg yolks

3 cups all-purpose flour

3/4 teaspoon salt

1/4 cup sugar

1/2 cup finely chopped almonds

1/2 cup butter

1 cup dark brown sugar

1 cup broken pecans

Back in 1954, when this recipe was the talk of the town, everyone wasn't on the fast-paced time schedule they are in the 90s. But treasured comfort foods are returning. Consider these fragrant rolls to put together Saturday night and to bake Sunday morning.

Soften yeast in cream. Soften butter and add egg yolks, flour, salt and yeast mixture. Beat until dough leaves sides of bowl. Chill overnight. Roll out thin on a board dredged with sugar and almonds. Roll up and cut in 1/2-inch slices.

Melt butter in 9-by-13-inch baking dish, sprinkle with brown sugar and pecans. Place dough spirals, cut side down, on pecans. Let rise until doubled. Bake in 375-degree oven for 30 minutes. Turn out at once.

Baked Caramel Corn

Yields 6 quarts

1 cup butter

2 cups brown sugar, packed

1/2 cup light or dark corn syrup

1 tablespoon salt

1/2 teaspoon baking soda

1 tablespoon vanilla

6 quarts popped corn

Peanuts, or other nuts, if desired

Children will be impressed that this crunchy old-time snack is homemade. They may expect it to be served in a red and white box with a prize. It's that close to Cracker Jack. If the syrup is left to boil and not stirred, as the directions state, no candy thermometer is needed. Accompaniments are shiny red apples.

Melt butter. Stir in brown sugar, corn syrup, and salt. Bring to a boil, stirring constantly. Then boil for 5 minutes without stirring. Remove from heat. Stir in soda and vanilla.

It is easier to divide corn and nuts, mixed together, into two batches and pour the hot syrup over each. Mix with two large spoons.

Turn into two large, shallow pans. Bake 1 hour in 250 degree oven. Cool before breaking apart and store in a tightly covered container. During the baking, the popcorn can be stirred every 15 minutes for a more even distribution of the caramel coating, but it is not necessary.

Dog Cookies

Yields about 24

1/2 cup all-purpose flour

1 cup whole wheat flour

1 cup dry skim milk

1/3 cup quick cooking oats

2 tablespoons wheat germ

1/3 cup vegetable oil

1 large egg, beaten

2 beef or chicken bouillon cubes, dissolved
    in 1 tablespoon hot water

1/2 cup water

The recipe for these crunchy treats was canine-tested before it was published for dog lovers everywhere. Neighborhood pets were invited to a tasting set up on a red and white-check covered table on the lawn. The cookies disappeared in seconds, and the furry tasters looked for more. If ever the food editor puts a product on the retail market, it won't be salsa, jams, or noodles, but these cookies. She joined in the tasting. They were pretty good.

Combine flours, milk powder, oats, wheat germ, oil, egg, bouillon, and water in food processor, or in mixing bowl. Mix well and form into a ball.

Divide ball into 2 parts. Knead one piece for about a minute and roll out on a lightly floured surface to 1/2-inch thickness. Cut with a small biscuit cutter. Place 6 biscuits on a 9 or 10-inch microwave-safe plate. Cook on 50% power for about 6 minutes, until firm. Roll out remaining piece of dough and the scraps left from cutting the biscuits, cut, and cook.

Or bake all biscuits at once for 15 minutes in 350-degree oven. Makes about 24, depending upon the size of the cutter. A small size is suggested. Refrigerate.

Matzo Dumplings

1/3 cup rendered chicken fat or

vegetable oil

1 cup matzo meal

Salt and pepper

Dash nutmeg

3 eggs, beaten

2 quarts water

1 tablespoon salt

Matzo balls floating in clear chicken broth are a picture to behold, and eating them brings even more pleasure. This recipe was featured during Passover in 1986, but everyone should try them, at any season. They may even cure a winter cold.

Blend fat or oil with matzo meal and seasonings. Stir in eggs. Bring water to a boil, add salt. Form mixture into small balls.

Drop from tablespoon into boiling water; simmer for 20 minutes. Serve in hot chicken broth.

Easy White Bread

2 cups all purpose flour,

    plus another 4 to 5 cups

¼ cup sugar

1 tablespoon salt

2 packages dry yeast

2¼ cups milk

¼ cup cooking oil

1 egg

Please, no bread machines. This everyday bread is made by the time-honored hand-kneading method that is guaranteed to be therapeutic in today's fast-paced lifestyle. Be a good neighbor. Take a loaf next door.

Combine 2 cups flour, sugar, salt, and yeast. Heat milk with oil over low heat until warm. Add it and beaten egg to flour mixture. Beat ½ minute at low speed, 3 minutes at medium speed. Gradually stir in another 4 to 5 cups of flour to form a soft dough. Knead about 1 minute on floured surface; longer won't hurt.

Place in a greased 2½-quart bowl and turn dough over to grease all sides. Cover and let rise in warm place until double, about an hour.

Punch down and shape into 2 loaves. One of the most successful ways to shape dough into loaves is to roll each portion into a 7-by-14-inch rectangle. Starting with 7-inch side, roll up tightly, jelly-roll fashion. Turn ends under and seal before placing seam-side down in pan. This process releases air. Place in greased pans. Cover and let rise in warm place until light, about 45 minutes.

Bake 40 to 45 minutes in 350-degree oven until loaf sounds hollow when tapped. Remove from pans immediately and brush with butter.

High Performance Dough

1 envelope active dry yeast

½ cup sugar

2 eggs, lightly beaten

1 teaspoon salt

1 cup milk

½ cup butter

4 cups flour

Pizza? Cinnamon rolls? Crescent rolls? This dough performs in all three styles. It is a basic, easy-to-do standby that encourages novice yeast bakers.

Mix all together in large bowl. Cover with plastic wrap or a clean towel and let rise overnight, or make early in morning and let rise during the day.

Divide dough into three balls to make three varieties or use all of dough for one.

TO MAKE CRESCENT ROLLS: Roll each ball into a circle and cut into eighths. Roll each triangle, from wide end to point. Place on cookie sheet; cover with clean towel, and let double in size. Bake 10 minutes in 400-degree oven.

TO MAKE CINNAMON ROLLS: Roll each ball into rectangles. Spread with butter, cinnamon, brown sugar, and chopped nuts. Roll up lengthwise and slice into 12 rolls. Arrange in 8-inch cake pan; let double in size, bake 20 minutes in 400-degree oven.

TO USE AS PIZZA DOUGH: Press half a ball into 8-by-13-inch greased pan. Cover with pizza toppings and bake 10 minutes in 425-degree oven.

Four-Grain Walnut Bread

Yields 3 loaves

1 cup quick-cooking oatmeal

2 cups water

1 tablespoon salt

1/4 cup molasses

1/4 cup butter

2 packages active dry yeast

1 1/4 cups lukewarm water

1 cup rye flour

1 cup whole wheat flour

1/2 cup wheat germ

1/2 cup bran flakes

1/2 cup fine-grain yellow cornmeal

1 cup walnuts, finely ground

Unbleached all-purpose flour

Oats, wheat, rye, and corn produce a fascinating texture in a health bread. Bakers will be pleased that this recipe makes three loaves. They won't last long!

Combine oatmeal and the 2 cups water in a saucepan and bring to a boil. Remove from heat. Place in a mixing bowl the salt, molasses, and butter; pour the oatmeal mixture over them. Let cool to lukewarm. Sprinkle yeast into 1/2 cup of the lukewarm water and let stand until dissolved. Then add the dissolved yeast and remaining 3/4 cup of water to the oatmeal mixture, beating until smooth.

Add rye flour, whole wheat flour, wheat germ, bran flakes, and cornmeal; beat until smooth. Mix walnuts into the dough. Gradually add enough white flour to make a soft dough. Turn out on a lightly floured board and knead until smooth and satiny.

Place in a bowl, cover, and let rise in a warm place until doubled in size. Punch down and turn out on a lightly floured board. Divide into thirds and shape each piece into a loaf. Place in three greased 9-by-5-inch loaf pans. Cover and let rise until doubled in size.

Bake in a 375-degree oven for 35 to 40 minutes or until the loaves sound hollow when thumped. Remove from pans and let cool on a rack.

Marcy Kaptur's Polish Coffee Cake

Yields 2 coffee cakes

1 envelope dry yeast

1/2 cup warm water or warm orange juice

1 cup milk, scalded, then cooled
    to lukewarm

1/4 pound butter

3 eggs

3/4 cup sugar

1/2 teaspoon nutmeg

1 tablespoon grated orange rind

1/2 cup raisins, soaked in hot water and
    drained

4 cups flour

Topping:

1 beaten egg for glaze

5 tablespoons flour

2 tablespoons butter

2 tablespoons sugar

1/8 teaspoon nutmeg

Congresswoman Marcy Kaptur's allegiance to family traditions and homespun foods from back home are spotlighted at fund-raising bake sales held in Toledo. Hundreds of yeast Polish coffee cakes are baked by campaign supporters. Miss Kaptur comes home from Washington, D.C. to join the baking marathon. This is the Kaptur family recipe.

Lightly oil 2 (8-by-5-inch) loaf pans.

Dissolve yeast in water or orange juice. Scald milk and add butter and stir until it melts.

Beat eggs and sugar. Add milk with butter, nutmeg, and orange rind. Stir in drained raisins; beat well. Stir in dissolved yeast and beat well again. Gradually add flour and continue to beat until dough is pliable. It will be sticky.

Divide dough into 2 portions. Knead each piece on floured surface and add more flour, little by little, as necessary. Place in prepared pans, cover, and let rise 2 hours in warm place until double in size.

Punch dough down and knead again lightly. Form each into loaf shape. Return to loaf pans. Cover and let rise again to double in size, from 1 to 2 hours.

Combine topping ingredients. Brush loaves with beaten egg and sprinkle them with topping mixture. Bake 35 to 40 minutes in 350-degree oven.

photo on cover

Onion-Poppy Seed Braid

Yields 1 loaf

Bread:

1 package active dry yeast

1/4 cup warm water

4 1/2 to 5 cups flour

1/4 cup butter, melted

1 cup warm milk

1/4 cup sugar

1 3/4 teaspoons salt

1 egg, beaten

Filling:

1 cup chopped onion

1/4 cup butter, melted

3 tablespoons poppy seeds

1/4 teaspoon salt

1 egg, beaten, for glaze

Additional poppy seeds

Wrapped around a savory onion filling, this is a bread to serve with bowls of hot soup or with sliced ham. Fair warning: it's for advanced bakers who know the ropes and how to braid them.

In large bowl, dissolve yeast in warm water. Add 2 cups flour, melted butter, milk, sugar, salt, and 1 egg. Beat at medium speed 2 minutes. With wooden spoon, stir in enough additional flour to make a stiff dough, about 2 cups. Spoon onto lightly floured surface and knead until smooth and elastic, about 8 to 10 minutes. Place in greased bowl; turn to grease top. Cover and let rise in warm place, free from draft, until doubled in bulk, about 1 hour.

In small bowl, combine onion, melted butter, poppy seeds, and salt. Set filling aside.

Punch dough down. On lightly floured surface, roll dough into a 20-by-8-inch rectangle. Cut in half from 8-inch side, forming two 20-by-4-inch rectangles. Spread onion filling onto each to within 1/2 inch of edges. Fold 20-inch sides together. Pinch seams to seal, forming two long ropes. Twist the ropes together. On lightly greased baking sheet, form dough into a ring. Cover and let rise in warm place, free from draft, until doubled, about 1 hour.

Brush dough ring with remaining egg. Sprinkle with additional poppy seeds. Bake in a preheated 350-degree oven 40 minutes or until bread sounds hollow when tapped. Cool on wire rack.

Pita Bread

2 packages dry yeast

1/4 teaspoon sugar

2 cups warm water

1/4 cup olive oil

1 1/2 tablespoons salt

6 cups hard wheat flour, or more

Cornmeal

Middle Eastern pocket bread has gone mainstream for all ages. The round bread discs that tear open to form a pocket are handy containers for all types of fillings, from savory meat combinations to crisp salads. In Toledo, we like to spoon hummus and fatoosh into the pockets, and children don't complain of they find a pita peanut butter sandwich in their lunches.

Place yeast, sugar, and 1/2 cup water in mixing bowl and let stand until yeast dissolves. Add remaining 1 1/2 cups water, oil, salt, and 5 cups flour, 1 cup at a time, mixing vigorously after each addition. The dough will be sticky.

Turn out onto floured board and work in the remaining 1 cup flour, or more if dough is still sticky. Knead for 10 minutes until dough is smooth and elastic. Shape in a ball and place in an oiled bowl and turn to coat dough. Cover and let rise about 2 hours, until doubled.

Punch down. Turn out onto a floured board and let rest 10 minutes. Divide into 8 equal pieces and shape each into a ball. Cover balls with a clean towel and let rest 30 minutes.

Flatten each with a well-floured rolling pin and roll to 1/8-inch thickness into 8-inch circles. Dust 2 baking sheets with cornmeal and place 2 circles on each sheet. Cover and let rest again for 1/2 hour. Leave the other circles, covered, on lightly floured surface.

Uncover bread on first baking sheet. Place it on lowest rack of 500-degree oven. Do not open door for 5 minutes, then move it to a higher shelf and continue baking 3 to 5 minutes, until loaves are puffed like balloons and lightly browned. Repeat until all loaves are baked. They will deflate when cooling.

Salted Rye Braids

Yields 2 loaves

5 cups unsifted white flour, or more

2 cups unsifted rye flour

1 tablespoon salt

1 tablespoon caraway seeds

2 packages fast rising yeast

1 tablespoon butter, softened

2 1/2 cups very hot tap water,
    to 130 degrees

Cornmeal

1 egg white, beaten with 1 tablespoon
    cold water

Caraway seeds

1 teaspoon coarse salt

The aroma of homemade bread filtering through the house is gratifying to both baker and family members. Here, salted rye braids are crested with caraway seeds.

Combine flours. In a large bowl, thoroughly mix 3 cups of flour mixture with salt, caraway seeds, and undissolved yeast. Add softened butter.

Gradually add water to dry ingredients and beat 2 minutes at medium speed of electric mixer. Scrape bowl occasionally. Add half the flour mixture, or enough to make a thick batter.

Beat at high speed 2 minutes. Stir in additional flour mixture to make a soft dough. Turn out onto lightly floured board; knead until smooth and elastic, about 8 to 10 minutes. Place in greased bowl, turning to grease top. Cover and let rise in warm place, free from draft, until doubled, about 45 minutes.

Punch down dough. Turn out onto lightly floured board. Divide dough in half; divide each half into 3 equal pieces. Roll each piece into a rope 18 inches long. Braid 3 ropes together. Seal ends, tuck underneath.

Place on greased baking sheet which has been sprinkled with cornmeal. Repeat with remaining ropes. Cover and let rise until doubled, about 45 minutes. Bake in a 400-degree oven for 20 minutes. Remove from oven. Brush with beaten egg white and water.

Sprinkle with caraway seeds, then with coarse salt. Return braids to oven. Bake 5 minutes longer. Remove from baking sheets and cool on wire racks.

Swedish Limpa

2/3 cup molasses

2½ cups water

2/3 cup brown sugar, firmly packed

1 tablespoon anise seed

2 teaspoons salt

¼ cup butter

4 teaspoons grated orange rind

1 envelope yeast

½ cup lukewarm water

4 cups sifted rye flour

5½ cups sifted all-purpose flour

Melted butter

In the chain of international breads which reaches around the world, limpa is a valuable link. It's distinctive because of the anise and molasses that rye flour absorbs admirably. No margarine here, please. The Swedes, as do all Scandinavians, use butter.

Mix molasses, 2½ cups water, brown sugar, anise seed, and salt in saucepan. Bring to a boil, then cook gently, uncovered, for 5 minutes. Remove from heat. Add butter and orange rind. Let stand until lukewarm.

Dissolve yeast in ½ cup lukewarm water. Add cooled molasses mixture and mix well. Stir in rye flour. Beat until smooth. Cover and let rise at room temperature about 1 hour. After the dough has risen, add 5 cups all-purpose flour and sprinkle remaining ½ cup flour on pastry cloth or board.

Knead dough until smooth and elastic. Place in greased bowl. Cover and let rise 2 to 3½ hours or until double. Punch down dough. Shape into loaves and put in bread pans. Let rise again until double. Bake 45 to 55 minutes in 350-degree oven. Remove from pans and brush with melted butter.

Tender Dinner Rolls

Yields 2 dozen

2 tablespoons shortening

1 teaspoon salt

¼ cup sugar

1 package yeast

1 ½ cups lukewarm water

3 ½ cups flour

1 egg, well beaten

Melted butter

Lucy Howe and her husband, Jim, operate Howe's Kountry Kettle near Hudson, Michigan. By dawn's early light and a hot oven, Lucy turns out breads, rolls, and apple dumplings that are hallmarks of the small country cafe.

Add shortening, salt, sugar, and yeast to lukewarm water and stir until the shortening is melted. Stir in flour and mix to a soft dough. Cover and set in a warm place to rise, about 1½ hours. Punch down dough and add beaten egg. Knead lightly on floured board; form dough into a ball. Cover again and let rise in warm place.

Roll out dough to ½-inch thickness. Cut into rounds with a 2-inch biscuit cutter. Crease centers and brush with melted butter. Fold over and seal edges. Place rolls on lightly greased baking sheet. Brush again with melted butter and sprinkle with sesame seeds. Let rise to double in a warm place. Bake 20 minutes in 400-degree oven.

 # Desserts

We are counting fat grams and carrying pocket-size calorie counters. We faithfully attend exercise class and are buying more fruits and vegetables than ever before.

To be sure, Americans are aware of diet vs. health risks. We read product labels, and we are living longer.

Such evidence does not mean we have given up desserts. Response to The Blade food pages which feature dessert recipes and the dessert recipe contests are proof of the pudding. Desserts have not lost grace.

Midwesterners have an insatiable sweet tooth that is satisfied by a myriad of cakes, pies, and cookies made from recipes that have been passed through generations. Sugar, peanut butter oatmeal, and molasses cookies are every day fare, baked with love and butter and sugar. The pick-your-own strawberry season is well-attended in fields throughout the area. Berries that are piled high in baskets go into all sorts of sweets and jams. Our strawberry pie and strawberry trifle recipes are ones not to miss. Apple pie is the Ohio favorite, but when peaches and cherries are ripe in local orchards, they move into the spotlight as the chosen fillings.

We continue to favor cobblers, fruit crunches, and pound cake.

The dessert selections reach around the world to Australia for its beautiful, light-as-air Pavlova and to Hungary for a recipe for butter pastry. Then we come back home for local specialties. Maumee River Mud Cake is named for the river on which Toledo is located, and Mud Hen Bars are named for the city's baseball team.

On opposite page: Strawberry Cream Roll brings together angel food cake, whipped cream, and fresh berries (page 222)

Butter-Rich Pound Cake

Serves 12

1 1/2 cups butter

1 (8-ounce) package cream cheese

3 cups sugar

2 teaspoons vanilla or another

    flavoring

2 eggs and 1 cup flour, beaten well

Pound cakes are of British origin and are named literally. After cup cakes were named because the ingredients were measured in cups, bakers named the cake made in pounds: one pound of sugar, one pound of butter, one pound of eggs—the pound cake. The secret to enjoyment of this rich pound cake is to eat slim slices and not fuss about the butter and eggs.

Cream butter, cream cheese, and sugar well and add vanilla flavoring. (If lemon flavoring is preferred, use 1 teaspoon of lemon flavoring plus the grated rind of 1 lemon.) To the creamed mixture, add each of the two eggs beaten with 1 cup flour. Add them separately, and incorporate well each time an addition is made.

Bake in a bundt pan which has been sprayed with a vegetable non-stick product. Bake in a 300-degree oven 1 hour and 20 minutes, or until a toothpick comes out clean. Let cool in pan 45 minutes before turning out on serving plate.

When cool, sprinkle with powdered sugar.

Individual Cheesecakes

Yields 18 servings

18 vanilla wafers

4 (3-ounce) packages cream cheese,
softened

2/3 cup sugar

2 eggs

1 teaspoon vanilla

1 cup sour cream

1/3 cup sugar

1 3/4 cups sliced strawberries

Statistics are in. People are not turning away from desserts, but they appreciate smaller portions. Small cheesecakes baked in muffin tins are one answer. The crust is a vanilla wafer. The topping can vary with the seasons, from strawberries to blueberries to raspberries, and on and on.

Line 18 muffin pans with paper liners. Place a vanilla wafer in each cup. Beat cream cheese until light and fluffy; gradually beat in 2/3 cup sugar. Add eggs and vanilla and beat well.

Fill muffin cups 2/3 full. Bake 10 minutes in 350-degree oven. Cool.

Combine sour cream and 1/3 cup sugar. Divide and spread over each cheesecake. Top each with a heaping teaspoon of sweetened strawberries. Freeze until firm. Remove from freezer 5 minutes before serving.

First Grand Prize Italian Cream Cake

Serves 12

1/2 cup butter

1/2 cup shortening

1 3/4 cups sugar

5 eggs, separated

2 cups cake flour

1/2 teaspoon salt

1 teaspoon baking soda

1 1/2 cups buttermilk

1 cup chopped pecans

1 teaspoon vanilla

1 1/2 cups coconut

1/4 cup more sugar

Additional chopped pecans
      and coconut

A three-layer cake made from scratch stands tall with a cream cheese frosting. The five-egg, buttermilk light batter is studded with pecans and coconut. Chris Davidson, Maumee, Ohio, received the top prize in The Blade Holiday Recipe contest in 1982 with this entry.

Cream butter and shortening. Add sugar and egg yolks and beat well. Sift flour, salt, and soda. Beat into butter mixture. Slowly add and beat in buttermilk and vanilla. Beat 2 minutes with electric mixer. Stir in pecans and coconut.

Beat egg whites until soft peaks form and slowly add the 1/4 cup sugar; beat to a soft meringue. Carefully fold into first mixture with a wire whisk or with a wooden spoon.

Divide batter among 3 greased and floured 9-inch cake pans. Bake 30 minutes in 325-degree oven. Let stand in pans about 10 minutes before removing. Fill and frost layers with cream cheese frosting while cake is slightly warm. Top cake with additional coconut and pecans.

CREAM CHEESE FROSTING: Combine 12 ounces softened cream cheese, 6 cups powdered sugar, 1 1/2 teaspoons vanilla, 1/2 cup soft butter; beat until fluffy.

Maumee River Mud Cake

4 eggs

2 cups sugar

1 cup melted butter

1½ cups flour

⅓ cup cocoa

1 teaspoon vanilla

1 cup coconut

2 cups chopped pecans or walnuts

1 (7-ounce) jar marshmallow cream

Only Nancy Crew, Napoleon, Ohio, knows how many recipes she has submitted to Blade-sponsored contests. But everyone knows she picks the best ones to enter. Here is a cake, complete with a floodtide frosting. It is named for the river which flows through northwest Ohio. Despite the name, this is a delicious cake.

Combine eggs and sugar in mixing bowl and beat at high speed 5 minutes. Combine butter, flour, cocoa, vanilla, coconut, and nuts in another bowl. Combine the two mixtures and mix well. Pour into greased and floured 9-by-13-inch pan.

Bake 30 minutes in 350-degree oven or until it tests done. Remove from oven and spread with marshmallow cream. Let set for a few minutes before frosting, but apply frosting while it is still warm.

FLOODTIDE FROSTING: Combine ½ cup melted butter, 6 tablespoons milk, 1 pound confectioners' sugar, 1 teaspoon vanilla, and 2 cups chopped nuts. Spread carefully over marshmallow cream.

Pavlova

12 egg whites

1 1/2 cups superfine sugar

1/2 teaspoon vanilla

1 teaspoon white vinegar

1 teaspoon cornstarch

4 tablespoons boiling water

Filling:

1 1/4 cups whipping cream

1 tablespoon powdered sugar

Sliced kiwifruit and strawberries

Once Australian Pavlova has been admired and tasted, there is no mystery why it is named for the Russian ballerina, Anna Pavlova. The classic dessert is as light as a ballerina's pirouette and as frothy as a tutu. It is particularly lovely and authentic when topped with vivid green kiwifruit slices.

Place egg whites, superfine sugar, vanilla, vinegar, cornstarch, and boiling water in medium bowl and beat with electric mixer until smooth, stiff, and glossy, about 10-12 minutes.

Place a sheet of baking parchment, or waxed paper, on cookie sheet. Brush lightly with melted butter and dust with a little cornstarch. Spoon prepared meringue mixture onto the prepared tray to form a 9-inch circle. Bake in the center of the oven for 10 minutes at 350 degrees; reduce heat to 300 degrees and bake an additional 45 minutes. Cool in oven before removing from tray.

Whip cream and powdered sugar until stiff and spread over cooled meringue layer. Top with sliced kiwifruit and, for more color, sliced strawberries.

Piña Colada Tropical Cake

1 package white cake mix
    for 2-layer cake
1 (3-ounce) package instant coconut
    cream pudding and pie mix
4 eggs
1 cup cold water
¼ cup oil
⅓ cup 80 proof dark rum

Filling and frosting:

1 (8-ounce) can crushed pineapple
    with juice
1 (3-ounce) package coconut cream
    instant pudding and pie filling mix
⅓ cup dark rum
1 (9-ounce) container frozen whipped
    topping, thawed
1 cup flake coconut

This is one of the favorite recipes that came from the late 1980s The Best Cooks in Town series, when Blade readers were invited to submit names of good cooks they knew. Marian Stokes, Sandusky County recorder, lives in a large brick farm house with a country kitchen. The day The Blade food editor and photographer visited Mrs. Stokes and her husband, Dan, the kitchen was filled with good things to eat, including this cake.

Blend cake mix, pudding mix, eggs, water, oil, and rum in large mixer bowl and beat 4 minutes at medium speed. Divide batter between 2 greased and floured 9-inch cake pans. Bake in 350-degree oven 25 to 30 minutes. Remove from pans and cool.

To make filling and frosting, combine crushed pineapple, pudding mix, and rum. Mix to blend. Fold in topping and coconut. Fill and frost cake. Sprinkle with additional coconut, if desired.

Popcorn Cake

1 (7-ounce) jar marshmallow creme

½ cup butter

3 quarts popped corn

1 pound package small gumdrops
in many colors

½ pound peanuts, or other nuts

A fun dessert for a child's birthday party or a picnic, this is a no-bake treat studded with gum drops and peanuts packed in a tube pan. Et voila! It slips right out. The afternoon two cakes were taken to be photographed in front of a merry-go-round at a local shopping center, they were almost eaten before the picture could be taken. Everyone wanted a taste.

Melt marshmallow creme and butter. Put popped corn in large bowl and mix in gumdrops and nuts. Pour melted marshmallow creme mixture over and mix well with hands.

Pack tightly into buttered tube pan and let stand overnight before unmolding onto serving plate.

Sponge Cake for Cake Rolls

9 large eggs, separated

1 teaspoon cream of tartar

1½ cups sugar

1 teaspoon orange flavoring

Grated rind of 1 orange

1 cup potato starch, also called

    potato flour

½ teaspoon salt

It may take several practice runs before a cake roll is perfected. But once the baker can turn out a tender cake roll, the choice of fillings can follow the seasons, from strawberries in June to peaches in August, raspberries in September, and bananas any time of the year.

Thoroughly grease and line with brown paper a 13-by-17-inch jelly-roll pan. Beat egg whites until foamy. Add cream of tartar and very gradually, 1 tablespoon at a time, ¾ cup sugar. Continue beating until thick and shiny. Set aside.

Beat egg yolks until thick. Add remaining sugar, orange flavoring, and rind, and continue beating until thick. Beat in potato starch, mix with salt until the batter is smooth. Fold part of egg whites into the yolk mixture. Then, very carefully, fold this mixture into the remaining egg whites.

Pour mixture into pan and spread evenly with spatula. Bake at 375 degrees for about 20 minutes. Remove from oven and let cool slightly. Turn out onto sugar sprinkled foil or waxed paper and roll up like a jelly roll. Let cool completely before unrolling and filling.

One way to use the cake roll is with bananas and whipped cream filling. Whip 2 cups heavy cream until thick, adding ½ cup sugar and 1 teaspoon vanilla. Combine 1 cup whipped cream with 4 sliced bananas. Spread filling on unrolled sponge cake and roll up. Use remaining whipped cream to ice cake roll. Sprinkle with pecans.

Strawberry Cream Roll

1 (14½-ounce) box angel food cake mix

2 tablespoons flour

1 pint fresh strawberries

1 tablespoon powdered sugar

1 pint whipping cream, whipped

"This is from a mix? Wow! May I have the recipe?" Expect similar compliments from friends who are served this luscious angel roll, filled and rolled with fresh strawberries and whipped cream. It's truly a winner.

Lightly grease 15-by-10½-by-1-inch jelly roll pan and line with waxed paper. Prepare cake mix according to package directions, and spread in prepared pan. Bake 15 to 17 minutes in 375-degree oven or until firm to the touch. Do not overbake.

Sift flour on a clean towel. Loosen cake and turn out onto towel. Peel off waxed paper which is now on top of the cake. Carefully trim browned edges of cake with serrated knife.

Roll cake in towel from narrow end. Cool on wire rack, seam side down, for 20 minutes. Meanwhile, clean berries, retain a few whole berries for garnish. Slice remainder and add powdered sugar to them. Whip cream until soft peaks form. Set aside 1½ cups whipped cream. Fold sliced strawberries into remaining whipped cream.

Unroll cake. Spread strawberry-whipped cream mixture evenly over cake, cut side up. Roll cake from narrow end with mixture inside. Place seam side down on serving plate. Frost with reserved whipped cream and garnish with strawberries. Chill at least 2 hours before slicing.

photo page 212

Wine Cake

1 standard box yellow cake mix

1 large package instant vanilla

    pudding mix

4 eggs

3/4 cup oil

3/4 cup light sherry

1 teaspoon nutmeg

This cake, made from a mix, has been treasured since 1964, when this recipe was found in the night stand drawer in a room the food editor occupied after surgery at The Toledo Hospital. It had been left by a thoughtful nurse and has been made at least four times a year since, always with a grateful memory of its source.

Mix all ingredients and beat on medium speed 5 minutes. Grease and flour a 10-inch tube pan. Bake 45 to 55 minutes in 350-degree oven. Cool 5 minutes before turning out onto cake plate. Sprinkle with confectioners' sugar.

Cherry Coconut Bars

Yields about 4

Crust:

1 cup flour

1/2 cup butter

3 tablespoons powdered sugar

Topping:

2 eggs

1 cup sugar

1/4 cup flour

1/2 teaspoon baking powder

1/4 teaspoon salt

1 teaspoon vanilla

3/4 cup chopped nuts

1/2 cup coconut

1/2 cup chopped maraschino cherries

Do men bake cookies? That was the question asked for a December, 1994, story. Sure enough, the answer was yes, and several men were anxious to share recipes. Each reported that his mother encouraged him to learn to cook and bake when he was growing up. A sample of Milt Whitmer's butter-rich cherry-coconut cookies was a real favorite. Do cut them into small squares.

To make the crust, combine all ingredients with hands and pat into 8-by-8-inch pan. Bake 20 to 25 minutes in 350-degree oven.

To make the topping, beat eggs. Stir in remaining ingredients in the order given. Spread evenly over baked crust. Bake an additional 25 minutes in same temperature oven.

Cool before cutting into small squares.

Fruitcake Cookies

1 1/2 cups brown sugar

1 cup butter

3 well-beaten eggs

1 1/2 teaspoons vanilla

1 teaspoon baking soda

2 1/2 cups flour

1/2 pound blanched almonds

1/2 pound Brazil nuts or pecans

1 pound English walnuts

1/2 pound candied cherries

4 slices candied pineapple

2 pounds dates

These are so easy to make and keep moist because of all the nuts and fruits. Even though fruitcakes have taken a rap in recent years, these cookies will be well-received.

Finely cut nuts and fruits. Cream butter and sugar. Add eggs and vanilla. Mix well. Sift dry ingredients and stir in. Mix in nuts and fruits. Place teaspoonful portions on well-greased cookie sheet. Bake 12 to 15 minutes in 350-degree oven, until golden. Be careful not to burn.

Joe E. Browns

1 pound butter

1 pound light brown sugar

11 eggs

1 pound chopped pecans

½ cup all purpose flour

½ teaspoon salt

1 teaspoon vanilla

Rose Naftalin named these rolled cookies after comedian Joe E. Brown, a Toledo native. Mrs. Naftalin gained a legion of fans for all manner of baked goods when she operated a delicatessen. She moved to Portland, Oregon, in 1955, but old-timers still talk about Rose and the deli. If they can find it, young bakers can get acquainted through her cookbook, <u>Grandma Rose's Book of Sinfully Delicious Cakes, Cookies, Pies, Cheesecakes, Cake Rolls, and Pastries.</u>

Cream butter and sugar, and beat until light and fluffy. Add eggs, 1 at a time, beating after each addition. Stir in pecans, flour, salt, and vanilla. Drop batter by teaspoonfuls onto greased cookie sheets. Put only 4 cookies on sheet at a time and be sure to beat the batter each time some is used.

Bake about 12 to 15 minutes in a 350-degree oven, until light brown. Remove each cookie with metal spatula and roll up like a cigar. If cookies get too brittle to roll, return to oven for a few minutes and again start rolling. The process is a little slow at first, but as you continue to work, you'll become proficient, and it will go much faster. When cooled, be sure to keep these cookies in a covered can.

Molasses Cookies

1½ cups vegetable shortening

2 cups sugar

½ cup molasses, unsulphured

2 eggs

4 cups sifted all-purpose flour

4 teaspoons soda

2 teaspoons cinnamon

1 teaspoon cloves

1 teaspoon ginger

1 teaspoon salt

Molasses has been a favored flavoring of American cooks dating back to Boston baked beans, gingerbread, shoofly pie, Indian pudding, and good old-fashioned cookies like these. You'll be sorry if you cut the recipe in half. Six dozen cookies may not be enough.

Cream sugar and shortening. Add molasses and eggs; beat well. Sift dry ingredients and stir into first mixture. It will be a stiff dough. Cover and chill, overnight if desired.

Form into 1-inch, or larger, balls. Dip tops and turn in granulated sugar. Bake 2 inches apart on greased cookie sheet 9 minutes in 375-degree oven.

Mud Hen Bars

½ cup shortening (part butter)

1 cup sugar

1 whole egg

2 eggs, separated

1½ cups flour

1 teaspoon baking powder

¼ teaspoon salt

1 cup chopped nuts

½ cup semisweet chocolate chips

1 cup miniature marshmallows

1 cup light brown sugar, packed

Not every baseball team has a high-scoring cookie recipe named in its honor. This one is for the Toledo Mud Hens, the top farm team for the Detroit Tigers. It has a meringue topping baked onto a rich marshmallow-chocolate chip base.

Cream shortening and white sugar. Beat in whole egg and 2 egg yolks. Sift flour with baking powder and salt. Combine creamed and dry mixtures and blend thoroughly. Spread batter in lightly greased 9-by-13-inch pan. Sprinkle chopped nuts, chocolate chips, and marshmallows over batter.

Make meringue topping by beating the whites of the 2 separated eggs until they are stiff, then folding brown sugar into the egg whites. Spread meringue evenly over top of batter.

Bake 30 to 40 minutes in 350-degree oven. Cut into bars when cooled.

Old-Fashioned Sugar Cookies

Yields 8 dozen

1 cup butter

1 cup vegetable oil

1 cup granulated sugar

1 cup powdered sugar

1 teaspoon vanilla

2 eggs

1 teaspoon baking soda

4 cups flour

1 teaspoon cream of tartar

1 teaspoon salt

As tender as love, and that's what they are made of, along with the essentials that make a rich cookie. Eight dozen? You'll make a double batch of these the next time. Grace Robinson often brought these mouth-watering cookies for office birthday celebrations at The Blade.

Thoroughly cream butter, vegetable oil, and both sugars. Add vanilla and eggs; beat well. Sift dry ingredients; stir in and blend.

Roll a teaspoon of dough into a small ball. Place on a lightly greased cookie sheet and press down with the bottom of a glass tumbler which has been dipped in sugar. Repeat with remaining dough. Bake 12 minutes in 375-degree oven.

Soft Orange Cookies

2 cups white sugar

2 cups butter

4 eggs

1 (6-ounce) package orange-flavored
   gelatin

2 teaspoons baking soda

6 cups flour

1 teaspoon baking powder

1 cup milk

Vanilla and almond flavorings

Erma Yoder, a young mother of four children, lives in Kidron, Ohio, the largest Amish settlement in the United States. The Yoders are committed to the Amish lifestyle. The family travels by horse and buggy. Erma's sparkling white laundry is hung out of doors to dry. The day Erma shared this recipe in late August, she was making school dresses and shirts for the children. Three bushels of peaches were on hand to be canned. When she turned cookbook pages to select a recipe for her Toledo friend, the children said, "Give her that one." That's the story behind this drop cookie recipe, which is flavored and tinted with orange gelatin.

Cream sugar and butter; beat in eggs. Combine gelatin with soda, flour, and baking powder. Add alternately with milk. Stir in flavorings. Mix well.

Drop from teaspoon onto lightly oiled cookie sheet. Bake in 350-degree oven for about 10 minutes.

Peanut Butter Oatmeal Cookies

1 cup firmly packed brown sugar

3/4 cup sugar

1 cup butter

1 cup peanut butter

2 eggs

2 cups flour

1 cup rolled oats

2 teaspoons soda

1/2 teaspoon salt

Every mother and grandmother needs an old-fashioned cookie recipe like this one. Keep the book handy for frequent repeats.

Combine first 5 ingredients; blend well. Stir in remaining ingredients. Drop by teaspoonful, 2 inches apart, onto ungreased cookie sheet.
Press each with a fork. Bake in 350-degree oven 8 to 12 minutes until golden brown. Remove from cookie sheet.

Raspberry Meringue Squares

3/4 cup butter

1/4 cup sugar

2 large egg yolks at room temperature

1 1/2 cups all-purpose flour

1 cup raspberry preserves

1/2 cup flaked coconut

2 reserved egg whites, at

    room temperature

1/2 cup sugar

1 cup finely chopped walnuts

Raspberries and chocolate, the compatible dessert couple of the 90s, bake harmoniously in this butter-rich bar which is topped by meringue.

In large bowl, cream butter with 1/4 cup sugar until fluffy. Beat in egg yolks. Stir in flour until well-blended. Spread evenly on bottom of greased 9-by-13-inch pan. Bake 15 minutes in 350-degree oven, or until golden.

Spread raspberry preserves over layer in pan. Sprinkle coconut over preserves. Beat egg whites until soft peaks form. Slowly beat in 1/2 cup sugar until peaks are stiff and glossy. Spoon meringue over coconut and sprinkle with nuts. Bake 25 minutes in 350-degree oven until lightly browned.

Cool before cutting into bars. If the knife is dipped into hot water, it will cut more easily.

White Velvet Cut-Outs

1 pound butter

1 (8-ounce) package cream cheese at
    room temperature

2 cups white sugar

2 egg yolks

1 teaspoon vanilla

4½ cups flour

The Blade's most popular cookie recipe is made with cream cheese. It rolls out smoothly. Cut-outs are associated with the Christmas season, but this one can be cut into shapes for all seasons, and decorated accordingly.

Cream butter and cream cheese, preferably with a mixer. Add sugar, egg yolks, and vanilla. Beat until well-mixed. Gradually incorporate flour and mix well. Cover and chill several hours, or overnight.

Roll out on a lightly floured board and cut into desired shapes. Do not roll this dough too thin; it is tender. Bake on lightly greased sheets 10 to 12 minutes in 350-degree oven, being careful not to overbake. Frost and decorate as desired.

Fruit Filled Hungarian Butter Pastry

Yields 4 to 4½ dozen

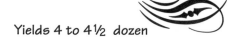

½ pound butter, softened

3 cups flour

1 teaspoon salt

2 teaspoons baking powder

1 cup sugar

6 egg yolks

1 cup sour cream

Apricot, cherry, or another

    canned filling

6 egg whites

Toledo's rich ethnic heritage is well-represented at the International Institute of Toledo. The several nationality group affiliates share food culture by giving luncheons and recipe demonstrations. This recipe for pastry that rolls out like silk was demonstrated at an institute affair.

Add flour to butter in mixing bowl and, with hands, crumble and mix. Add salt, baking powder, and sugar; continue to crumble with hands. Add egg yolks and sour cream and mix well. Separate dough into two parts.

Roll out one half on floured board to fit large baking pan. Place in pan and spread filling evenly over it with a spatula. Roll out other half of dough and place on top of filling. Cut criss-cross slashes on top of dough.

Bake in 350-degree oven 25 minutes. Beat egg whites stiff; spread over baked pastry. Bake another 10 minutes until top is lightly browned. If desired, sprinkle with ground nuts mixed with sugar. Cut into squares.

Food Processor Pie Crust

Yields 2 (10-inch) and 1 (9-inch) shells

1 teaspoon salt

3 heaping cups flour

1 cup cold shortening

7 tablespoons ice water

The food editor's mother was an expert pie baker. From apple, custard, and elderberry to pumpkin and green tomato mincemeat, her repertoire was long. The pull-out bin in the pantry held 50 pounds of flour, and rarely were her boarders without a choice of pies. It was daily dessert. She cooled the pies on a shelf on the back porch. Occasionally one, or two, would be missing. She would scream, "What happened to my pies?" But she knew, as did everyone, that the tramps who lived in the dump down the street were aware of Mrs. Powell's good pies and of her generosity. This is not her recipe; she used lard, and she didn't have a food processor. This recipe is for the 90s. It works beautifully and, hopefully, will encourage young people to explore the pleasure of pie baking.

Use metal blade in food processor. Put flour and salt in processor bowl. Cut shortening into 3 pieces and add. Process until mixture gathers into pea sizes. Be careful and do not over-process.

Divide dough into 3 parts. Chill slightly. Either roll out between 2 sheets of waxed paper or on heavily floured board. If the counter is dampened, the waxed paper won't slide.

The Blade's Best Strawberry Pie

Yields 1 (10-inch) pie

1 quart strawberries

½ teaspoon salt

½ cup cold water

A few drops red food coloring

3 tablespoons cornstarch

1 cup sugar

1 (10-inch) pie shell, pre-baked

Strawberry picking time is a wonderful season. Families make it an adventure to go into the fields and fill baskets high with the luscious red berries that are fuller-flavored in Ohio and Michigan than they are in any other state. Naturally, strawberry pie recipes are numerous. This is the one that has been published by demand many times.

Wash and hull berries; remove and crush 1 cup. Mix with salt, water, and food coloring in saucepan. Mix cornstarch with sugar and stir into crushed berries. Cook over medium heat and stir until mixture comes to a boil and thickens. Remove from heat and allow to cool 30 minutes to an hour.

Place remaining whole berries in baked pie shell. Pour cooled sauce over. Refrigerate until filling sets.

Bob Hope's Lemon Pie

Serves 6

1 cup plus 2 tablespoons sugar

3 tablespoons cornstarch

1 cup boiling water

4 eggs, separated

4 tablespoons fresh lemon juice

2 tablespoons butter

Pinch of salt

Grated rind of 1 lemon

1 (8-inch) baked pie shell

A kind deed can become an embarrassment. When Bob Hope's advance man dropped off this lemon pie recipe in 1976, two days before the comedian's appearance in Toledo, the food editor decided to make a pie, following the recipe, and take it backstage. It is an Ohio recipe. Mr. Hope's mother made it when the family lived in Cleveland, and his wife, Dolores, baked it for special occasions. The pie was a beauty and was delivered to the doorman at the University of Toledo Centennial Hall as planned. The food editor's mistake was not to stay for the performance. When Mr. Hope came on stage, he announced her name, spotlights were shown throughout the auditorium, but Mary Alice Powell was not there to take a bow.

Combine cornstarch and sugar. Add boiling water slowly and stir constantly until thick and smooth over low heat. Remove from heat, beat egg yolks slightly. Continue to stir while adding egg yolks, lemon juice, butter, salt, and grated rind. Return to low heat and stir and cook 5 minutes. Cool.

Pour into baked shell. To make meringue, beat 3 egg whites with 2 tablespoons sugar, or more. Bake in 350-degree oven until meringue is lightly browned, about 10 minutes.

Butter Pecan Tarts

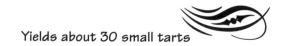

½ cup butter

1 cup light brown sugar

½ teaspoon salt

1 beaten egg

½ cup chopped pecans

Pastry

When we arrived at the home of Ruth Dudley, a prominent Findlay, Ohio, hostess, the side-board and the dining room table were covered with beautiful pastries. A concord grape pie garnished with single berries arranged as a bunch is memorable, but these tarts are a lot easier to make.

Cream butter and sugar. Add salt and beat until fluffy. Add egg and mix thoroughly. Fold in nuts.

Fill pastry-lined tiny tarts about ¾ full. Bake 20 to 25 minutes in 325-degree oven.

Green Tomato Pie

Serves 6

1 (9-inch) pie shell and pastry for top

4 to 5 cups thinly sliced

    green tomatoes

1½ cups sugar

¼ teaspoon salt

3 tablespoons flour

2 tablespoons minute tapioca

Grated rind of 1 lemon

½ cup fresh lemon juice

2 tablespoons butter

It is curious that people wait until the end of the tomato season to gather green tomatoes when they are always available before the fruit turns red. Green tomato mincemeat, pickles, and pie are midwestern specialties.

Place tomatoes in pie shell. Combine sugar, salt, flour, and tapioca, and spoon over tomatoes. Sprinkle lemon rind and lemon juice over all. Dot with butter. Place top crust over and seal. Cut slits in top.

Bake 15 minutes at 425 degrees. Reduce heat to 350 degrees and bake another 30 minutes. The pie should set several hours to allow filling to set. Serve at room temperature.

Ginger Peach Pie

6 to 8 fresh peaches, pared, pitted,

   and sliced

3 tablespoons flour

1/4 teaspoon ground ginger

1/4 teaspoon cinnamon

1 cup sugar

1/3 cup brown sugar

Pastry for 2 crust, (10-inch) pie

Ginger and peaches are compatible in this fresh pie filling. Please make it with a lattice top crust to let the beautiful color shine through.

Spoon peaches into 10-inch pie shell. Toss with flour to coat well. Combine remaining ingredients and sprinkle over peaches. Top with top crust, or make a lattice top. If a lattice top is not used, cut slits in top crust to vent.

Bake 10 minutes in 400-degree oven; reduce heat to 325 degrees and bake about 45 minutes to a golden brown.

Key Lime Cheese Pie

Serves 8

6 ounces softened cream cheese

1 (8-ounce) container frozen

    dessert topping

¼ cup sour cream

¼ cup lime juice

1 can sweetened condensed milk

1 (9-inch) graham cracker crust

No doubt about it, the heartland is pie country. We bake cakes for special occasions and cookies for parties and the children, but the dessert that always seems to fit is pie. This is so true that The Blade sponsored a pie baking contest in 1991. The winner, according to a panel of food professionals, was Kim Koepfer, whose pie fit the times, with ingredients which are on hand in many homes and go together quickly.

In a large bowl, whip cream cheese. Mix in dessert topping with whisk and add other ingredients. Beat at medium speed 1 minute. Spoon into pie shell and chill.

If desired, decorate the top of the pie with additional dessert topping fed through a pastry tube.

Lynn's Grasshopper Pie

1¼ cups fine chocolate wafer crumbs,

    approximately 20(2-inch) wafers

½ cup melted butter

½ cup milk

20 marshmallows

1 cup heavy cream, whipped

3 tablespoons green creme de menthe

3 tablespoons white creme de cacao

You just never know who's reading your column. When this liqueur-laced pie recipe from Lynn's Restaurant was published, a representative of the Ohio liquor control board telephoned the food editor to ask if the pie were served to minors at the restaurant. The light dessert in a chocolate crust is flavored with a small amount of creme de menthe and white creme de cacao.

Combine crumbs and melted butter. Press onto sides and bottom of 9-inch pie plate. Chill.

Heat milk in top of a double boiler over boiling water. Add marshmallows and stir until they are melted. Cool thoroughly.

Combine whipped cream, creme de menthe, and creme de cacao. Fold into cooled marshmallow mixture. Pour into chilled crumb crust. Chill until firm.

PINK SQUIRREL PIE: Substitute creme de almond for green creme de menthe.

GOLD CADILLAC PIE: Substitute galliano for green creme de menthe.

Ohio Champion Cherry Pie

1¼ cup sugar

¼ cup cornstarch

1 (20-ounce) frozen dry-pack pitted

    red tart cherries, 4 cups

¾ teaspoon vanilla

½ teaspoon almond extract

2 tablespoons butter

1 or 2 drops red food coloring (optional)

Pastry for 2 (9-inch) pie crusts

The pie that was declared America's best in the 1991 National Pie Celebration was baked by Diane Cordial, Powell, Ohio. The 50 contestants were judged champion bakers at their state fairs before the national event. Mrs. Cordial enters 150 baked items at the Ohio State Fair and brings home about 50 blue ribbons each year.

Combine sugar and cornstarch in medium heavy saucepan. Gently stir in cherries. Cook and stir on medium heat about 10 minutes, until mixture comes to a boil and is thickened and clear. Remove from heat. Stir in vanilla, almond extract, butter, and red food coloring, if desired.

Cool 1 hour before spooning into pie shell. Top with second crust and seal edges. Cut slits in top.

Bake 35 to 40 minutes in 375-degree oven.

Pumpkin Mousse Ice Cream Pie

1 1/4 cups crushed gingersnap cookies, about 28

1/3 cup butter, melted

1/4 cup sugar

1 pint vanilla ice cream

1 cup canned pumpkin

3/4 cup more sugar

1 1/2 teaspoons pumpkin pie spice

1 cup whipping cream

1/2 teaspoon vanilla extract

Open the freezer and there it is, ready to be served; an ice cream pie in a gingersnap crust with a creamy pumpkin topping.

Combine crushed cookies, butter, and sugar in small bowl. Press onto bottom and sides of 9-inch pie plate. Bake 8 minutes in preheated 375-degree oven. Cool.

Soften ice cream; spread over gingersnap crust. Freeze until firm.

Combine pumpkin, sugar, and pie spice in medium bowl. Beat cream and vanilla in small mixer bowl until stiff; fold into pumpkin mixture. Spoon over ice cream. Freeze until firm.

Sour Cream Apple Pie

2 tablespoons flour

1/8 teaspoon salt

3/4 cup sugar

1 egg, unbeaten

1 cup sour cream

1 teaspoon vanilla

1/4 teaspoon nutmeg

3 to 4 cups apple slices

1 unbaked (9-inch) pie shell

<u>Streusel topping:</u>

1/3 cup sugar

1/3 cup flour

1 teaspoon cinnamon

1/4 cup butter

To know how many kinds of apple pie there are in Ohio, you would first have to know how many bakers there are. Each person gives his pie a personal touch. Sour cream is often used in custard fillings. Note to cholesterol watchers: only one egg is called for.

Sift together 2 tablespoons flour, salt, and 3/4 cup sugar. Add egg, sour cream, vanilla, and nutmeg. Beat to a smooth, thin batter. Stir in apples. Pour into pastry.

Bake in 400-degree oven for 15 minutes, then reduce heat to 350-degrees and continue baking for another 30 minutes.

Combine 1/3 cup sugar, 1/3 cup flour, cinnamon, and butter. Sprinkle over hot pie; return to 350-degree oven and bake for 10 minutes to brown.

photo on cover

Walnut-Crumb Apple Pie

1 (9-inch) pie shell, unbaked

½ cup flour

½ cup light brown sugar, packed

½ teaspoon nutmeg

½ teaspoon cinnamon

½ cup butter

½ cup chopped walnuts

½ teaspoon baking soda

½ cup boiling water

¼ cup light molasses

1 (20-ounce) can sliced apples,
   drained, or 2½ cups fresh
   sliced apples

Consider tasting and judging more than 50 apple pies. That's the day breakfast, lunch, and dinner are skipped. It has happened more than once to The Blade food editor in apple country, where pie contests are as anticipated in the fall as are bright leaves and brilliant chrysanthemums. This recipe scored the highest in a 1984 contest. Walnuts and molasses give it interesting texture and flavor, and it's a one-crust pie. Those are always easier to make than a two-crusted one.

Combine flour, sugar, and spices. Cut in butter until mixture has a crumbly consistency. Mix in nuts. Turn half of the mixture into the unbaked pie shell.

In a large bowl, dissolve baking soda in boiling water. Add molasses and apples. Pour apples on top of flour mixture in pie shell. Cover with remaining flour mixture.

Place on cookie sheet in 400-degree oven and bake 40 minutes .

Refreshing Raspberry Ginger

3 (10-ounce) packages frozen raspberries,

    defrosted and well-drained,

    or 2 pints fresh

1½ pints heavy cream, whipped

1 cup brown sugar

½ teaspoon ground ginger

This lovely raspberry refreshment deserves to be served in the best stemware. It is light, with a delicate ginger flavor. Now that fresh raspberries are more available, substitute them for frozen berries. Consider passing a tray of shortbread.

    Gently separate berries. Whip cream until stiff. Mix sugar with ginger and gently fold into cream. Fold in berries lightly so as not to crush. Chill at least 1 hour.

    Before serving, stir gently to blend in any juices that have come from the berries.

Almond Dacquoise with Amaretto Cream

Serves 12

1½ cups finely ground almonds

1¼ cups sugar

1½ tablespoons cornstarch

6 egg whites

¼ teaspoon cream of tartar

⅛ teaspoon salt

1 teaspoon vanilla

¼ teaspoon almond extract

Amaretto butter cream

Whole and sliced almonds

When guests rave about this, don't blush and say, "Oh, it was nothing." Take every deserved bow for the stacked almond meringue layers filled with amaretto butter cream. It is wonderful, and it is work.

Combine almonds, 1 cup sugar, and cornstarch. Butter and flour 2 baking sheets; mark a 9-inch circle on each.

Beat egg whites foamy; add cream of tartar and salt. Continue beating. When peaks form, add ¼ cup sugar. Beat in extracts. Gently fold in ¼ of almonds at a time. Evenly spoon onto 9-inch circles. Bake at least 3 hours in 250-degree oven until layers are dried and browned. Slip onto wire racks to cool.

Place 1 layer on serving plate; spread with ⅔ of the amaretto cream to within ½ inch of edge. Sprinkle with ¼ of the almonds. Top with second meringue layer. Pipe remaining almond cream into rosettes. Dust with cinnamon. Garnish with whole and sliced almonds.

AMARETTO BUTTER CREAM: Beat 3 egg yolks and 1¼ cups powdered sugar until thick. Heat ¾ cup milk just to boiling. Remove from heat; beat some milk into yolk mixture and mix well. Pour it all back into saucepan; beat. Place over medium heat and stir until slightly thickened, 10 minutes. Do not boil.

Return to bowl and beat until cool. Beat in 1½ cups butter, one tablespoon at a time, at high speed. Add 3 tablespoons amaretto and 1 teaspoon almond extract. Makes 3 cups.

Apple and Cheese Crumble

4 large, tart cooking apples

½ cup sugar

1 teaspoon ground cinnamon

2 tablespoons water

Topping:

1 cup flour

½ cup sugar

1 teaspoon salt

1 cup sharp Cheddar cheese, shredded

½ cup melted butter

This is a dessert the food editor had forgotten about until she began the search for recipes for this book. It's a goodie from the 50s which honors the age-old belief that every piece of apple pie should be accompanied by cheese. It is simply a nice recipe, quickly put together. The sweetened apple slices are on the bottom, and the cheese is on the top.

Pare, core, and slice apples. Place in buttered 8-inch square baking dish. Combine the sugar and cinnamon, sprinkle over apples, add water.

Mix topping ingredients to crumbly consistency and spread evenly over apples. Bake 45 minutes in a 325-degree oven.

Carrot Charlotte

6 large eggs, separated

1/4 teaspoon salt

1 cup sugar

1/2 cup matzo meal

1 1/2 cups finely grated carrots

1/2 cup blanched almonds, ground fine

2 tablespoons blackberry wine

Shredded carrots and ground almonds add density to this Passover cake made with matzo meal. The recipe is from Joan Levitan, Toledo, who adds blackberry wine for a good measure of flavor.

Beat egg whites with salt until stiff, but not dry. Beat egg yolks until thick and lemon-colored. Gradually add sugar, but continue to beat as sugar is added. Fold in matzo meal, grated carrots, almonds, and wine. Fold and mix in beaten egg whites. Pour into greased 2 1/2-quart baking dish.
Bake 50 minutes to 1 hour in 350-degree oven.

Classic Tiramisu

Serves 8

6 egg yolks

1 1/4 cups sugar

1 1/4 cups mascarpone cheese

1 3/4 cups heavy whipping cream

2 (3-ounce) packages ladyfingers

1/3 cup amaretto or

    brandied espresso (below)

Sweetened whipped cream (below)

Grated semi-sweet chocolate, or cocoa

As soon as the light dessert layered with mascarpone cheese and ladyfingers began to appear in Italian restaurants, readers began to ask how to prepare it at home. This is the recipe we came up with and, according to Italian friends, it's on target.

In a small mixer bowl, beat yolks and sugar until thick, at least 1 minute. Spoon into top of double boiler over boiling water. Reduce heat to low; stir constantly 8 to 10 minutes. Remove from heat. Add mascarpone cheese; beat well. In small mixer bowl, beat whipping cream to stiff peaks form. Fold into egg yolk mixture. Set aside.

Line bottom and sides of 2 1/2-to-3-quart trifle bowl (glass and straight sided) with ladyfingers. Brush with amaretto or brandied espresso. Spoon half of yolk-cream mixture over ladyfingers in bowl. Repeat ladyfingers and brush them with amaretto or espresso. Spoon cream layer over. Garnish with sweetened whipped cream and sprinkle cocoa or grated chocolate over. Cover and refrigerate several hours or overnight.

A SUBSTITUTE for mascarpone cheese: In large mixing bowl, beat 1 (8-ounce) package cream cheese, 1/4 cup sour cream, and 2 tablespoons heavy, or whipping cream, until blended and fluffy.

BRANDIED ESPRESSO: If espresso coffee is not available, in small bowl, combine 1/3 cup hot water and 2 teaspoons instant coffee granules. Stir until coffee is dissolved. Blend in 1 teaspoon brandy.

SWEETENED WHIPPED CREAM: In small mixer bowl, beat 1/2 cup whipping cream. 1 tablespoon powdered sugar, and 1/4 teaspoon vanilla extract until stiff peaks form.

Creme de Menthe Ring

8 ladyfingers, split and cut in halves

2 quarts lime sherbet, softened

1/3 cup creme de menthe

1 pint strawberries, washed and hulled

Ladyfingers fence in lime sherbet laced with creme de menthe in this freezer dessert. The recipe suggests that the center of the mold be filled with strawberries, but other fruits can be used. Melon balls make a nice contrast to the green sherbet and, to keep the color coordinated, add some kiwi slices. Ladyfingers are not as easy to find as they once were. When you do find some, buy extra. They keep well, frozen, for months.

Line sides of 6½-cup ring mold with waxed paper and then with ladyfingers, rounded side out. Beat sherbet and creme de menthe until smooth, but not melted. Spoon into prepared mold; freeze until firm.

To serve, unmold and fill center with strawberries.

Drop Biscuit Peach Cobbler

½ cup sugar

1 tablespoon cornstarch

¼ teaspoon nutmeg

4 cups peeled, sliced fresh peaches

1 teaspoon lemon juice

1 cup all-purpose flour

1 tablespoon sugar

1½ teaspoons baking powder

½ teaspoons salt

3 tablespoons shortening

½ cup milk

   With all due respect to Georgia, Ohio peaches are a real treat in late summer. That's when cobblers, bubbling with fruit and topped by short biscuits, are pulled from the oven. Can you believe it? Some folks pour cream over them or add a scoop of ice cream.

   Mix ½ cup sugar, cornstarch, and nutmeg in 2-quart saucepan. Stir in peaches and lemon juice. Cook over medium heat, stirring constantly, until mixture thickens and boils. Boil and stir 1 minute. Pour into ungreased two-quart casserole.
   To make the biscuits, stir together flour, 1 tablespoon sugar, baking powder, and salt. Cut in shortening and milk.
   Drop 6 spoonfuls of dough, well-spaced, onto hot fruit. Bake 25 to 30 minutes in 400-degree oven, until biscuits are golden brown. Serve warm.

Grand Marnier Soufflé

1 orange

½ cup raisins

¼ cup Grand Marnier

3 tablespoons flour

¾ cup milk

6 tablespoons sugar

4 eggs, separated

2 tablespoons butter

1 teaspoon vanilla

1 additional egg white

¼ teaspoon salt

½ teaspoon cream of tartar

A soufflé that bakes high, wide, and handsome is a sweet ending usually reserved for fine dining away from home. But you can do it at home and impress guests. This one extends the Grand Marnier essence with fresh orange juice and zest in a sauce. Just be sure everyone is seated and ready for the presentation, because soufflés wait for no one.

Grate orange rind and juice orange. Combine orange juice, rind, and raisins in saucepan. Bring to boil; add 1 tablespoon liqueur. Cover and set aside.

Butter 2-quart soufflé dish and sprinkle with sugar. Blend flour and ½ of milk in saucepan. Blend in remaining milk and all but 1 tablespoon of sugar. Bring to a boil and stir and cool 1 minute until thick. Cook 3 minutes before whisking in egg yolks, 1 at a time. Blend in butter, vanilla, and remaining 3 tablespoons liqueur.

Beat egg whites and salt. When foamy, add cream of tartar. Beat to soft peaks before adding remaining tablespoon of sugar; beat to stiff, glossy peaks. Fold ¼ beaten whites into sauce; gently fold in remaining whites. Pour all but ½ cup mixture into prepared pan.

Bake about 30 minutes in a 375-degree oven. Add reserved soufflé mixture to raisin-orange mixture; serve over hot soufflé portions.

Peach-Baked Apples

6 medium baking apples

¼ cup peach preserves

¼ teaspoon cinnamon

¼ cup apple cider or juice

¾ cup crumbled chewy oatmeal cookies

Two fruits double the pleasure of this light fruit dessert with a simple crumbled oatmeal cookie topping. If the topping is omitted, the peach-topped apples can be an accompaniment to pork or chicken.

Cut apples in halves and remove cores. Place in 9-by-13-inch baking pan, cut side up. Combine preserves, cinnamon, and cider or juice. Drizzle over apples. Cover pan tightly with foil.

Bake in 350-degree oven 30 minutes until apples are just tender. Sprinkle crumbs over top and drizzle with preserves mixture in bottom of pan. Bake another 5 minutes, uncovered. Serve warm or cold. For dessert, serve with frozen vanilla yogurt. As a side dish, omit the cookie topping, and serve with pork or chicken.

Pears Vermouth

6 ripe anjou pears

6 whole cloves

1 cup sugar

1/2 cup sweet vermouth

1/4 cup water

Few drops red food coloring

Whipped cream, if desired

Blushing fresh pears are flavored with vermouth and clove in a light, refreshing dessert. The pears are particularly lovely when they stand upright in colored stemware. A dab or two of whipped cream carries it to ecstasy.

Peel pears, leaving stems on, and keeping as perfect a shape as possible. Stick a whole clove into each pear. Combine remaining ingredients except whipped cream in 1½-quart glass casserole. Add pears, cover with glass lid.

Microwave on high 6 minutes. Baste pears, turn over, and cover again. Continue cooking on high until tender. Or poach pears in liquid in saucepan over medium heat.

Arrange in large bowl with sauce and serve, if desired, with whipped cream.

The Priest's Cherries Jubilee

Serves 8 to 10

2 (16-ounce) cans fancy, pitted

   bing cherries

2 tablespoons cornstarch

¼ cup cold water

¼ cup brandy or cognac

2 tablespoons grain alcohol

Vanilla ice cream

Some of our best recipes have come from Catholic priests, and this one is no exception. The Reverend James Say, who has served parishes in Toledo, Defiance, and Port Clinton, Ohio, is an exceptionally fine cook whose worldwide travels are reflected in his international menus. When a Father Say dinner is auctioned at parish fund raisers, the high bidders know the dessert will be Cherries Jubilee, prepared tableside by the host.

Drain juice from cherries. Set juice and cherries aside in two separate bowls. Mix cornstarch and water.

At tableside, in the blazer of a chafing dish, or in an electric skillet, bring cherry juice to a boil. Thicken with cornstarch and water. Add cherries and stir until they are heated through. Pour brandy or cognac over cherries. Then pour grain alcohol over cherries.

Dim the room lights and ignite the jubilee. When flames subside, immediately serve over ice cream.

Rhubarb Crunch

1 cup sifted flour

3/4 cup oatmeal

1 cup firmly packed brown sugar

1/2 cup melted butter

1 teaspoon cinnamon

4 cups diced rhubarb

1 cup white sugar

2 tablespoons cornstarch

1 cup water

1 teaspoon vanilla

Pulling a stalk of cherry red rhubarb, breaking off the sprawling green leaf, and taking a bite is an early spring exercise. Sure enough, it is intensely tart, enough to make you wince, but it is a tonic in the heartland. In the spring, there is nothing like rhubarb sauce, pie filling, cobblers, and crunches like this one with an oatmeal crust. Don't spare the sugar.

Combine flour, oatmeal, brown sugar, melted butter, and cinnamon. Press half of the crumb mixture into a greased 9-by-13 inch pan. Top with diced rhubarb.

Combine white sugar, cornstarch, water, and vanilla; cook until thick. Pour over rhubarb and top with remaining crumbs. Bake about 1 hour in 350-degree oven. Especially good served with ice cream.

Strawberry Cheesecake Trifle

2 (8-ounce) packages cream cheese

1 (8-ounce) carton sour cream

1 pint whipping cream

2 cups confectioners' sugar

2 teaspoons vanilla

1 teaspoon almond flavoring

1 large angel-food cake

1 quart sliced strawberries, reserve a few
   whole for garnish

¼ cup sugar, optional

A trifle bowl is required to show off this picture-perfect strawberry dessert. Fresh berries are layered with a rich, creamy mixture of angel food cake, cream cheese, whipping cream, and sour cream. No wonder it's the berries.

Beat cream cheese until it is softened. Beat in sour cream. In another bowl, beat whipping cream until soft peaks form. Stir into creamed cheese mixture. Stir in confectioners' sugar, vanilla, and almond flavoring.

Cut angel food cake into 2-inch pieces. Gently fold cake into creamed mixture. Sugar berries with ¼ cup sugar, if desired.

Using a deep glass bowl, layer creamed mixture and strawberries, beginning and ending with creamed mixture. Garnish top with whole berries.

photo on cover

Buckeye Candies

Yields 12

1 cup sifted powdered sugar

1/2 cup creamy peanut butter

3 tablespoons butter, softened

1 pound melting and dipping chocolate

    coating

Travel anywhere, U.S.A., and it is doubtful you will find edible buckeyes. These peanut butter fondant balls, partially dipped in chocolate, are made to resemble buckeyes, the nuts on the state tree of Ohio. The nut was named by pioneers, who saw a resemblance between the nut of the tree and the eyes of the buck deer. In 1988 the Ohio Department of Natural Resources planted buckeye tree groves in state parks in a "Save the Buckeye" program. Eating these candies won't deplete the environment.

In a mixing bowl, combine powdered sugar, peanut butter, and butter. Mix with electric mixer until very smooth. Shape into 1-inch balls. Set aside on baking sheet lined with waxed paper for 20 minutes to dry.

Melt chocolate coating. Spear each peanut butter ball with a toothpick and dip into chocolate, coating about half of it. Remove toothpick. Smooth over toothpick hole, if desired. Store in a cool, dry place.

Hazelnut Truffles

Yields 2 dozen

11 squares semi-sweet chocolate,

cut into pieces

1 square unsweetened chocolate,

cut into pieces

3/4 cup whipping cream

2 tablespoons butter

1 tablespoon hazelnut liqueur or coffee-

flavored liqueur

3/4 cup hazelnuts, ground fine

Such indulgence. Can you to eat just one? As if two kinds of chocolate, whipping cream, butter, and hazelnuts aren't enough to guarantee bliss, hazelnut liqueur is added. This recipe is from Colleen Goldberg, a local confection shop owner.

In a small saucepan over low heat, melt chocolates, stirring constantly. Remove from heat.

In another small saucepan, heat whipping cream and butter just to boiling. Stir cream mixture into chocolate mixture; blend well. Stir in liqueur. Refrigerate about 2 hours or until it is easy to handle. Stir occasionally.

Roll into 3/4-inch balls using hands or a small melon baller. Roll in nuts. Place in candy cup papers and refrigerate.

Sugared Nuts

1 beaten egg white

1½ teaspoons water

2 cups salted mixed nuts

1 cup granulated sugar

½ to 1 teaspoon cinnamon

This food treasure is a nice one to have tucked away to use as a hostess gift or when guests arrive unexpectedly. Mixed nuts pick up a sugary cinnamon-flavored coating.

Beat egg white and mix with water. Coat nuts with mixture. Mix sugar and cinnamon in another bowl and add to nut mixture. Stir to mix well.

Cover cookie sheet with brown paper, greased well with shortening. Spread nut mixture over paper. Bake 20 to 25 minutes in 325-degree oven. Nuts will puff up on top and have brown edges.

Allow to cool enough to handle before breaking apart. Store in jar or tin, covered. Keeps 3 to 4 weeks.

Wildwood Manor Candied Orange Peel

Yields 2 cups

2 cups orange peel, cut into strips

2 cups sugar

1 cup water

⅛ teaspoon salt

Additional sugar to coat

Candied orange peel is a signature food at afternoon tea at the Manor House at Wildwood Metropark in Toledo. People from miles around gather in the solarium at the prized mansion the first Friday of every month but July. Tea and an incredible assortment of sweets and finger sandwiches are prepared by the Cinderellas, an auxiliary group as skilled in baking as they are in hospitality. To a background of grand piano music and the Manor House gardens, guests relax, and, for a time, are convinced that all is bright and wonderful in the world outside. Marian Lindsey, a Cinderella for many years, is credited with the candied orange peel recipe.

California thick-skinned oranges are recommended. Cover strips with cold water; bring to a boil. Boil 5 minutes. Drain. Cover again with cold water. Bring to a boil again, and again boil for 5 minutes. Repeat a third time.

Combine sugar, water, and salt and bring to a boil until the sugar dissolves. Add peeling strips and cool until the syrup spins a thread and registers 225 degrees on a candy thermometer. Remove peel, piece by piece, and roll in granulated sugar. Place on waxed paper to dry.

INDEX

Our foods tell us who we are and where we came from.
This saying has been an inspiration in all my work.

Mary Alice Powell

To order additional copies of *Aren't You Going To Taste It, Honey*,
please send a check or money order for $9.95 for each copy,
plus $1.50 shipping to:

THE BLADE
Marketing Department
Attn: Mary Alice Powell Cookbook
P.O. Box 555
Toledo, Ohio 43697-0555

This book is also available over the counter at
THE BLADE, 541 N. Superior St., Toledo, Ohio
and in Toledo area bookstores. For other information
call The Blade Marketing Department at 419-245-6275.